BEST
SERVED
WILD

BEST SERVED WILD

REAL FOOD FOR REAL ADVENTURES

BRENDAN LEONARD & ANNA BRONES

GUILFORD, CONNECTICUT

FALCON®

An imprint of Globe Pequot

Falcon and FalconGuides are registered trademarks and Make Adventure Your Story is a trademark of Rowman & Littlefield.

Distributed by NATIONAL BOOK NETWORK

British Library Cataloguing-in-Publication Information available

Library of Congress Cataloging-in-Publication Data available

ISBN 978-1-4930-2870-2 (paperback)
ISBN 978-1-4930-2871-9 (e-book)

♾™ The paper used in this publication meets the minimum requirements of American National Standard for Information Sciences—Permanence of Paper for Printed Library Materials, ANSI/NISO Z39.48-1992.

Printed in the United States of America

CONTENTS

OVERNIGHT TRIPS

MULTI-DAY OUTINGS

INTRODUCTION

"HUNGER IS THE BEST SEASONING"

I WASN'T THE FIRST PERSON TO SAY THE PHRASE "HUNGER IS THE BEST SEASONING," but I'm one of the most fervent believers in the concept—exercising and earning the right to replace calories, I think, makes eating a joyful experience. I have, at least once, calculated how many slices of New York–style pizza I could mathematically justify eating by running a 50-mile ultramarathon. (For the record, I also calculated the number of Chicago–style deep-dish pizza slices justified by the same amount of running.)

I have run/hiked rim to rim in the Grand Canyon in a single day and promptly purchased two ice-cream cones on the South Rim to eat before even changing out of my running gear. I have downed decadent feasts in small towns at the feet of mountain ranges like the Tetons, the Wind Rivers, and the Sangre de Cristos after days or weeks of earning those calories—and fantasizing about them.

I have organized and packed way too many calories for day hikes, weekend-, and weeklong backpacking trips and thought for a second at the end of each trip, "Wow, I guess I could have left some of that food at home and not had to carry the extra weight."

And then I immediately thought, "Nah. What fun would that be?"

I find great joy in earning calories by moving myself under my own power in wild places and replacing those calories in the most satisfying way possible—whether that's cooking my own recipes over a camp stove or shopping for cookies that I know won't crumble in my backpack and breakfast burritos that will slowly thaw in my pack as I make my way to the top of a peak for lunch. Oh, and of course, what's a cookie break without coffee?

With *Best Served Wild*, we wanted to share this joy of eating in the outdoors, or "extreme picnicking," or whatever you want to call it when you're out there. There's a famous climbing saying that the late alpinist Alex Lowe first coined in an interview in 1993: "The best climber in the world is the one having the most fun."

Well, we agree with that wholeheartedly, whether you're climbing some gnarly peak in the clouds, kayaking down the coast, camping out of the back of your car for a weekend, or just going for a nice day hike to see if the wildflowers are out yet or if the leaves have started changing. And having the most fun means eating food you enjoy. I've been on long trips where food was a little light, and I prefer to err on the side of gluttony, or whatever word you use to mean "enough chocolate, coffee, and foods that taste so good I would eat them even if I weren't 10 miles from the nearest road with no other options at hand."

We've used that ethos to guide us in writing this book, including a range of recipes that you can make at home and take on one-day adventures, meals you can make when you're camping near your vehicle and weight isn't a concern, and meals to pack on longer trips where you're carrying everything in a backpack for several days and you want to pack the lightest-weight (but, again, tastiest) food possible.

Recipes, Not Rules

Keep in mind that this is a book of recipes, not a book of rules. You have enough of those in your day-to-day life. We want you to have fun, not feel restricted. The recipes we've assembled in *Best Served Wild* are open to your own personal interpretation.

If, for example, you want to cover every recipe in here with Sriracha or some other hot sauce, that's up to you. We recommend maybe not doing that with the pancakes, but again, to each his or her own. If you want to add fresh chopped vegetables to either of the chili recipes, by all means go for it. If you want to quit your job, sell all your possessions, empty your life savings, move into a van, and live in it while traipsing around the American West and writing poetry, well, neither of the authors of this cookbook is judging you.

You might notice that the recipes in here are vegetarian. That's because both of us are vegetarian, and that's the way we think about food. We're not that qualified to advise anyone how to cook meat. Instead, we designed recipes we believe work just fine without meat, but you should feel free to supplement and get as wild as you want when using this cookbook. If you want to add precooked chicken to the chilaquiles, please do. If you want to add bacon to the nachos, go for it. If it makes you feel better to wear a chicken suit and sing Flaming Lips songs while standing at your camp stove cooking all these things, you know what, it's your life. Your campground neighbors may look at you a little funny, but you do you.

As you're flipping through the pages of *Best Served Wild*, look for the frying pan symbol—that's the sign for a recipe we think works well with some improvisation on your end, whether it's precooked chicken, precooked bacon, Spam, seitan, or tempeh. Feel free to add whatever you think works.

The whole point of going camping is to escape from many of the restrictions and pressures we have at home in our daily lives, so keep that idea in mind out there. Go wild. But keep your food stored properly so you don't get visited by bears during the night. That's probably a little too wild. Bears are fascinating and awesome creatures, but they lack both table manners and empathy for the general well-being of nearby humans.

Cooking over a Fire

You'll notice that almost all the recipes in this book are cooked on a camp stove except Campfire Corn on the Cob (page 104). "Camp Stove Corn on the Cob" just didn't have the same ring to it.

The lack of campfire recipes is not because we are campfire averse—we love a good campfire. There's nothing better than a cup of hot chocolate in your hands and the smell of smoke seeping into your clothes. Really, our tendency to not cook over a campfire is because we're lazy; when we want to eat, we want to eat. For that, cooking on a camp stove is reliable and quick (not to mention you're not always in a place where a campfire is an option). Cooking over a campfire isn't a science. It's more of an art—one that can vary greatly depending on how big your fire is, what you're cooking in, etc. Sometimes things cook quickly; other times they don't. Really, you could call it the Zen of Campfire Cooking.

For those of you who happen to love the art of campfire cooking, there are plenty of recipes in this book that can be adapted to an open fire, such as Clean Out the Cooler Vegetable Sauté (page 111), Seven-Can Chili for Six People (page 82), and Home on the Free-Range Veggie Burgers (page 132).

We're not going to give you any fancy guidelines for campfire cooking because, really, it all comes down to common sense:

> Only make campfires in appropriate places. Respect fire bans, and please don't harvest wild wood when you're not supposed to.

> Use a proper cooking vessel that won't melt or explode if over a fire; cast iron yes, plastic no.

> Adjust cooking times accordingly.

> Stir regularly.

> Don't burn yourself when picking up a pan.

One thing is for sure: If you cook on a campfire, your dinner will be one hundred times more photogenic, and you'll get that hint-of-smoke flavor that chefs charge extra for.

Whether over an open fire or a camp stove, we hope you're as into outdoor cooking as we are. Have fun out there, and remember that eating well is a big part of having fun. And if you make it to the summit or get some cool photos, that's pretty cool too.

—*Brendan Leonard*

HOW USING ONLY ONE BURNER
MAKES YOU A BETTER COOK

COOKING WELL IN A FULLY STOCKED KITCHEN IS ONE THING. Cooking on a camp stove? An entirely different matter. On one burner, away from the modern comforts of our kitchens, you have to be scrappy. You have to simplify the list of ingredients and create shortcuts that get around the fact that you don't have hours to soak or boil something. You have to think about how to turn a dish that usually requires a few different pots and pans into a one-pot meal. You have to think about new ways to reuse basic ingredients and which spices are going to pack the biggest punch. In the wild, creativity is rewarded with flavor, an ability to make something out of seemingly nothing.

Cooking outdoors is first and foremost about keeping yourself and your counterparts well fueled for adventure. But if all you needed was to be well fueled, you could turn to spoonfuls of peanut butter throughout the day and instant, freeze-dried meals at night.

Cooking outdoors is a creative challenge. It's the act of working within constraints and managing to pull even the most basic of meals together. We get excited about a meal outdoors not just because it puts fuel in our stomachs, but because there is something special about cooking on one stove, with one pot. Outdoors, we are stripped to the essentials, far from fast food and fast life. Here, the experience is as meaningful as the end product.

After a long trip, returning to your kitchen can be both exhilarating and overwhelming. It feels good to use the oven to roast vegetables or bake a cake, and yet it's tempting to want to stick to the one-pot meal strategy. Get nostalgic enough, and you might even take out that camp stove to use as a vehicle for revisiting fond memories.

By cooking outdoors, you discover a newfound appreciation for simple things: fresh food, a burner you can actually regulate, a sink that's easy to do dishes in. Cooking outdoors makes you a better cook because it forces you to be more aware of the process and more engaged in it, not necessarily because you're food-crazed or recipe-obsessed, but because you have a better knowledge of what it takes to put a meal on the table, no matter the circumstances. Return home after a trip, and cooking a meal at home can feel almost too easy—like you're cheating.

Forget all those cooking shows with their quick tips and cooking shortcuts, and their branded gadgets that do everything and nothing at all. If you're cooking successfully on a camp stove, you're a better cook than most people out there. You have a heightened awareness of the value of food, that what you put in your system actually does matter. You're creative; you can use oats to make veggie burgers. Turn dried fruit into a fancy dessert? No problem.

Throw any culinary problem at an outdoor cook, and he or she is sure to be able to find a solution. Ultimately, that's what gives you power in the kitchen—your ability to make use of what you have and scrape together a meal, no matter what.

It doesn't matter if you only know how to make pasta; cooking outside makes you a better cook full stop. I am certain even Julia Child would agree.

—Anna

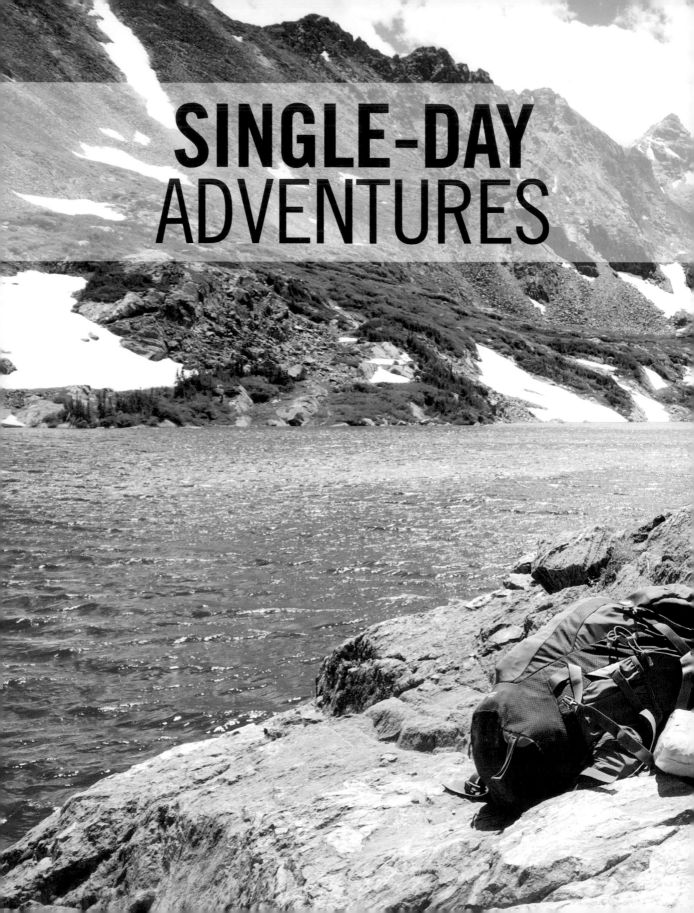

SINGLE-DAY ADVENTURES

NUTELLA CREPES
FOR PEAK BAGGERS WHO CAN'T MAKE CREPES

Do you like making crepes? How about at 4 a.m. before you leave for a hike to the top of a mountain? If you answered, "Of course not—that's ridiculous!" then this recipe is for you. It's basically the guts of a standard crepe recipe without the painful mixing of flour, sugar, salt, milk, eggs, and butter and pureeing all that in a blender.

Sacrifice a bit of texture and a small amount of taste (which you won't care about after you've been hiking for a while) by swapping the crepe outside for a large flour tortilla. After you eat this on a day hike, we promise you'll scream, "Peanut butter and jelly sandwiches are for SUCKERS!" Each crepe contains enough sweet chocolate to power you through the second half of the uphill portion of your summit mission, or to celebrate at the top after you've signed the summit register.

MAKES Enough for 1 person who is climbing a mountain today

INGREDIENTS

1 enormous gob of Nutella

1 large (aka burrito-size) flour tortilla

1 banana, sliced

1 handful of walnuts

OPTIONAL

Honey

Peanut butter

PREPARATION

Spread the Nutella over half the tortilla.

Arrange banana slices over the Nutella-covered side of the tortilla; place walnuts in the gaps between the banana slices.

Fold the naked half of the tortilla over the half with all the good stuff on it, like a quesadilla. Slice it in two triangle-shaped halves.

Place in a ziplock bag for later.

ADDITIONAL TIPS

> For enough sugar to give your pancreas the workout of its life, drizzle the Nutella, banana slices, and walnuts with honey just before you fold the tortilla.

> For more protein and fat with less sugar, spread peanut butter on the tortilla; add a streak or thin layer of Nutella over the top of that before adding the bananas.

NOTE You can make and eat these even if your hike doesn't involve a summit. You can make and eat them if you're not hiking, or even going outside anytime soon. It's a free country, isn't it?

PROTEIN BARS
THAT DON'T TASTE LIKE CHALK

Rumor* has it that protein is necessary for sustaining life. Believe the hype—you should eat protein when you're in the out-of-doors. If you can't find a protein-rich energy bar you like (or you'd just like to bask in the satisfaction of making your own), my friend Jayson has developed this recipe for bars that will give you that "I just ate a bunch of protein" full feeling you crave when you're out on the trail.

Feel free to experiment and add dried fruit or try different flavors of protein powder with this recipe if, for example, you don't like chocolate. Although if you don't like chocolate, what is wrong with you?

*also, science

MAKES About 24 (2 × 2-inch) protein bars. Basically, you could live off the contents of this pan for 3 or 4 days.

INGREDIENTS

2 cups peanut butter or almond butter

1½ cups raw honey

½ cup coconut oil

2¼ cups chocolate protein powder

3 cups regular oatmeal

1 tablespoon cinnamon

2 tablespoons raw cacao powder

½ cup raw pumpkin seeds or almond slivers

PREPARATION

Combine peanut (or almond) butter, honey, and coconut oil in a pot or pan, and warm it on a stove over low heat.

In a large bowl, mix the dry ingredients.

Add the warm and gooey peanut/almond butter, honey, coconut oil, and mix it thoroughly with the dry ingredients. You can try to use a wooden spoon or other implement, but you'll probably give up and just use your hands after a while. Don't be afraid. Get all up in your food. It's going to get all up in you sometime soon. If the mixture is crumbly, don't be afraid to add a few sprinkles of water.

Press the mixture into a 13 × 9-inch pan and place in your refrigerator. Keep the pan in the refrigerator for at least 1 hour.

Remove the mixture from the refrigerator and cut into bars the size of your choice.

Place in plastic bags before putting them in your backpack.

THE DIMINISHING RETURNS
OF THAT NEW ENERGY BAR FLAVOR
YOU'RE CURRENTLY EXCITED ABOUT

HEY, THAT NEW BANANABERRY CHOCO MOCHA CHIP WALNUT ALMOND PISTACHIO Cinnamon Vanilla Cardamom bar you just pulled out of your backpack—it's tasty, huh?

Yeah, compared to the other flavors of energy bars you've had recently, it's pretty OK. When you consider the other types of food you can toss in a backpack and hike for 6 or 10 miles, it's decent.

But let's be honest here. Have you noticed that there are approximately eleven billion different flavors and textures of energy bars in your local supermarket or outdoor gear store? Why is that?

Here's one idea: You can only tolerate a specific flavor of energy bar for a fixed amount of time. Some of them you can eat a dozen before you're sick of the flavor; some of them you can eat thirty or forty. I would argue that the maximum number of bars of a specific flavor that you can eat and still enjoy is around fifty. And then it falls off a cliff. One day you're out hiking and pull out your fiftieth Black Cherry Salted Cacao Nib Peanut Pretzel Truffle Oil bar of the year. You take a bite, and instead of enjoying the view from your lunch spot, you ask yourself: "What the hell am I doing with my life? Why am I eating something that sort of reminds me of food instead of just eating food? Would I be happier with a peanut butter and jelly sandwich?"

Hey, I don't want to tell you how to live your life, but consider taking some real food with you next time instead of taking the easy way out and filling your backpack with prepackaged food products hammered into squares or rectangles.

Don't get me wrong; energy bars have a place in the outdoors. They're an easy, compact way to add 250 to 400 calories to your food supply each day on a long backpacking trip and a good source of nutrients (and often fiber) on a long day hike in combination with your other snacks that taste good no matter what. But if you eat two of them every day of a three-day backpacking trip, or on a dozen day hikes in a row, you're probably going to start hating them. So consider some stuff that's closer to real food: slices of pizza, sandwiches, a box of leftover Chinese food from the other night, or a frozen breakfast burrito that will slowly thaw on your drive to the trailhead and hike to the summit. Or, you know, any of the recipes from the first section of this book.

You're often working hard in the outdoors—hiking up quad-busting trails, feeling your heartbeat pound inside your ears, and stopping every once in a while so you don't cough up a lung. Why not reward yourself with some decent food when you take a periodic break from all that? You've probably earned it. Don't ruin your snack breaks with food that's just easy to pack in lieu of being easy to love.

—Brendan

WB & J
(WALNUT BUTTER FOR WALNUT BUTTER AND JELLY)

We're all well aware that there's no trail lunch more iconic than peanut butter and jelly sandwiches. Well, except for maybe peanut butter and honey. But sometimes you have to break the rules.

We break the rules with this walnut butter, an easy-to-make-at-home nut butter that tastes almost like cookie dough. Really want it to taste like cookie dough? Throw in a handful of chocolate chips.

Since this recipe is made with raw walnuts, eventually it's going to go off, so don't plan on carrying it on extended trips. For a few days it will do just fine.

INGREDIENTS

2 cups raw walnuts

2 tablespoons honey

½ teaspoon salt

3–4 tablespoons oil (Use a lighter, more neutral-tasting oil, like safflower, unless you can afford walnut oil; in which case, do it.)

PREPARATION

Place the walnuts, honey, and salt in a food processor or blender. Pulse until you get a coarse mixture. Add the oil and puree until the mixture is thick and smooth.

Store in an airtight container.

BREAKFAST BURRITOS
YOU CAN EAT FOR ANY MEAL

Everyone knows that burritos are the preferred sandwich of the outdoor world. Self-contained, they travel well; and if you're adventuring with a friend, you can congratulate each other for getting to the summit with a trademark Burrito Fistbump. Breakfast, lunch, dinner: It's all a burrito time. This recipe is perfect for when you've got an early-morning start and want to eat breakfast on the way or at the trailhead. Just make the burritos the night before, stash them in your backpack in the morning, and you can have breakfast whenever you want. Burritos fit perfectly into bike jersey pockets, which makes them great fuel for long rides. You can also toss these in the coals of a morning campfire if you want to enjoy a warm burrito.

We use buckwheat in this recipe because rice is boring, but you can tweak this recipe depending on your tastes. Ditch the eggs and cheese if you need them to be vegan. Up the bean content if you're in desperate need of protein. Triple the hot sauce if that's your jam. Add new ingredients and make these your own!

MAKES 1 burrito

INGREDIENTS

Tinfoil (not to eat, of course)

1 large flour tortilla

About ½ cup cooked buckwheat

About ½ cup black beans, strained

1 egg, scrambled

2–3 tablespoons grated cheese

2 tablespoons salsa

Cilantro

MEAT OPTIONAL

PREPARATION

Tear off a piece of tinfoil that is a little wider than your tortilla. Place the tortilla flat on the tinfoil.

Evenly spread the remaining ingredients out toward the bottom of the tortilla (the side closer to you). Gently fold up the bottom as well as the sides, and roll the burrito together, making sure it's tightly wrapped within the tinfoil.

Pack. Burrito Fistbump with a friend. Eat.

WRAPPER-LESS
GRANOLA BARS

Everyone always complains about how granola bars shouldn't be considered healthy, given the amount of sugar in them. But forget your health for a second. Here you are enjoying the glories that Mother Nature has to offer, and you're busy stuffing single-use wrappers into your pocket. What kind of an outdoor lover are you?

There's a solution to your "I'm-having-a-negative-impact" woes: Skip the store-bought granola bars and make your own. Bake up a batch of granola bars pre-trip, and you can ensure that they will be 100 percent wrapper-less. Which means you can add as much dried fruit and chocolate as you want, since you've done your good deed for the day.

A lot of homemade granola bars are notorious for falling apart. There is an inevitable crumbliness to any homemade granola bar, but these are fairly firm and solid thanks to the glue created by peanut butter and honey.

The base recipe is easy to tweak according to what you want in your granola bars. Choose whatever nuts, seeds, or dried fruit you want. Don't want chocolate? Switch that out for more nuts and fruit. Some tasty combos: walnuts and figs, apricot and hazelnuts, sunflower seeds and cherries.

INGREDIENTS

2 cups rolled oats

½ cup chocolate chips

½ cup chopped nuts or seeds

½ cup cut-up dried fruit (small pieces)

¼ teaspoon salt

1 teaspoon ground cinnamon

½ cup peanut butter

½ cup honey

PREPARATION

Preheat the oven to 350°F.

In a large bowl, combine the oats, chocolate chips, nuts, fruit, salt, and cinnamon. Stir together.

In a saucepan over medium heat, melt the peanut butter and honey. When they have melted together, whisk together with a fork. Pour over the oat mixture, and mix together with a large wooden spoon until well-blended. Toward the end, this can get a little hard to mix together; crush any clumps with the wooden spoon to be sure there are no dry oats left.

Line a 9-inch square baking dish with parchment paper. Spread the mixture into the dish, using your hands or a spatula to evenly spread it out. Once spread out, firmly press the mixture down.

Bake for 20 to 25 minutes, until golden brown.

Remove from the oven and let cool completely. Once cool, gently remove the entire block from the pan by lifting the edges of the parchment paper. Place on a cutting board, and use a serrated knife to cut the block into small bars.

Store in an airtight container.

HOW TO
DRY YOUR OWN APPLES

Packing dried fruit on a trip is Adventuring 101. If you don't have at least one kind of dried fruit with you, can you really call it a trip?

On the list of Easy-to-Buy Dried Fruits, apples don't always come in at the top, which is a shame because they are delicious. Dried apple rings tend to be a little pricey, but good news apple lovers: You can make them at home, and you don't need a dehydrator.

Even better, you can add a little cinnamon to them to make this dried fruit extra special. Imagine a few slices torn up and added to your morning oatmeal. Or eaten as a celebratory snack for making it up a hill and to a good lookout.

Once you start drying your own apples, you'll never look back.

INGREDIENTS

2 small to medium apples (This is about what fits on a large baking tray.)

Ground cinnamon (optional)

PREPARATION

Preheat the oven to 200°F.

Rinse the apples. Using a knife, slice the apples horizontally as thinly as possible.

Line a baking tray with a silicone baking mat or parchment paper. Spread out the apple slices, making sure they do not overlap. Sprinkle with cinnamon, if desired.

Bake in the oven for about 1½ to 2 hours, until the apples are soft and tender, but no longer moist. Your baking time will depend on the thickness of the apple slices. You can flip the apples about midway and sprinkle the other side with cinnamon.

Remove apples from oven and let cool.

Store in an airtight container.

NOTE As the apples dry out, they will shrink a little bit, and you can easily remove the seeds once they're done.

COOL KIDS MAKE THEIR OWN SNACKS

OH, YOU BROUGHT *THAT* **BRAND OF ENERGY BARS?** How impressive.

You know what's more impressive? Making your own.

Stand in front of the snack section at any outdoor gear shop and you're sure to find a snack for any backcountry need. Full of Antioxidants So You Don't Get Cancer While Camping! Boosted with Protein So Your River Trip Is Actually Like Pumping Iron! Gluten-Free, Raw, Vegan, Made of Straw because Straw Is the New Superfood!

I mean, you can't climb a mountain if you don't have the right brand of food, right? How are you going to survive?

Here's the truth: Snacks aren't going to turn you into a superhuman. They might keep you from bonking, but beyond that, snacks are small pieces of food that tide you over until the next meal. They're really just an excuse to take a break when you're tired and want to stop. Instead, you take out a snack and tell yourself, "I've got to refuel right now so I can keep my energy levels at maximum efficiency."

When you're tired and hungry and you need to eat, it doesn't need to be a special bar, or a ball or a gel. It just needs to be ATTIE: A Thing That Is Edible.

Screw the designer snacks on the trail; the best snacks are the DIY kind you throw together at the house. A little peanut butter, a handful of oats, some honey, whatever dried fruit you have lying around; mix it up. If it doesn't form into anything transportable, place it in a plastic bag and eat it with a spoon.

With homemade snacks, you don't need to worry about being the jerk who drops granola wrappers on the trail. No one likes that guy.

How do you go about making your own snacks? Here's an easy guide.

What to buy:

Grab a few of your favorite designer snacks, turn them over, and look at the ingredients list. Here's a simple formula for making them at home: Buy all the ingredients you can pronounce; skip all the ones you can't. Oh, and probably add those chia seeds for good measure because, you know, superfoods are hot right now.

How to prepare:

Most bars or balls are some rendition of a sticky ingredient mashed together with a dry ingredient. That's it. Sure, your snacks might not look exactly the same as store-bought, but chances are no matter how much you paid for that high-end granola bar, it's still just a mixture of seeds, nuts and dried fruit.

Snacks that don't require preparation:

Some snacks don't even require preparation. Honey is Nature's energy gel, proven to taste good and make you feel even better; Mother Nature doesn't need a marketing campaign to tell you that. Love those fruit and nut bars? Surprise! They're just fruit and nuts. Grab some dehydrated fruit, your favorite kind of nut, and you're done!

—Anna

MAKE YOUR OWN
"NUTELLA"

Why would you want to make your own chocolate hazelnut butter when Nutella is easy to find at any grocery or convenience store? Well, here are a few reasons:

> Telling your friends "I made my own Nutella" wins you points.
> You can skip all that palm oil and soy lecithin nonsense.
> You can feel good about eating the entire batch, because it's pretty much just hazelnuts and cocoa powder.

Spread this DIY chocolate hazelnut butter on bread, mix it into oatmeal, or use it to make Three-Way Nut Butter. Another fun thing about making your own chocolate hazelnut butter? You can add stuff to it. Try a couple teaspoons of finely ground coffee for a mocha flavor, or add orange zest for something akin to those chocolate oranges everyone seems to buy around the holidays. In the mood for something spicy? A dash of chili powder will do the trick. And if you want to sweeten the spread without adding more sugar, throw in some vanilla extract or cinnamon.

INGREDIENTS

1 cup toasted hazelnuts

¼ cup unsweetened cocoa powder

½ teaspoon sea salt

2 tablespoons organic cane sugar or honey

2–4 tablespoons oil (Use a lighter, more neutral-tasting oil, like safflower, unless you can afford hazelnut oil; in which case, this is a must.)

PREPARATION

You can buy toasted hazelnuts or buy raw ones and toast them yourself. Toast in a baking pan at 350°F for 10 to 15 minutes, until they are a dark brown and the skins are cracking. During toasting, shake the pan a few times to get them evenly toasted.

Remove the hazelnuts from the oven and let cool for a few minutes until cool enough to handle. Leaving the skins on makes the spread a little more bitter (but still delicious). If you don't want that, you can place the hazelnuts in a clean tea towel and roll the tea towel with your hands to remove most of the hazelnut skins. You won't get all the skins off, but that's OK.

In a food processor, combine the nuts, cocoa powder, salt, and sugar; pulse until the mixture is coarse. Add the oil a little at a time, and puree until the mixture comes together and is smooth. How much oil you add will change the consistency of the chocolate hazelnut butter —a little less for a chunkier version; a little more for a runnier one.

Store in an airtight container.

"COOKING OUTDOORS IS A **CREATIVE CHALLENGE.**"

YOU DON'T NEED TO MEASURE
AN INFORMED RANT

TODAY'S AVERAGE WESTERN KITCHEN IS LESS A WORKING SPACE TO MAKE FOOD and more an exhibition for single-purpose gadgets that don't do much more than gather dust. The Quesadilla Maker 5000 (could have just used a frying pan), the 32x Bread Maker-o-Matic (could have just used the oven), and the Milkshak'ah (could have just used a blender) all seemed like such a good idea at the time. But now your kitchen counters are filled with good intentions, and little room to actually make food.

The camp kitchen is simplified. A few utensils, a stove, and a pot or pan are really all you need—the perfect reminder that when you get home, maybe you should host a garage sale. If nothing else, cooking outdoors reminds you that you need very little to make a solid meal.

But if you're a recipe lover, it might seem hard to live without your measuring cups in the great outdoors. How else are you supposed to figure out what 1¼ cup of couscous is? Good news: You don't need to.

Most of the recipes in this book come with measurements. Otherwise we probably wouldn't be able to get away with calling this book a cookbook. Instead it would be titled *Lists of Ingredients to Use for Dinner Tonight*. But truth be told, we rarely measure when we're cooking outdoors. Just as you don't need gadgets to make a good meal, you don't need precise measurements either. Throw them out! Free yourself from the shackles of measuring ingredients!

Baking can be a science, and that's why some of our bar and snack recipes to be made at home *before* you hit the trail are more precise. Backcountry cooking? Less so. In fact, it's highly unlikely that you will completely destroy a recipe no matter what you do, unless you dump in the entire container of salt or leave your camp stove to go and chat with the wandering campsite moose and burn the whole meal. Other than that, your meal is probably going to work itself out. You just need to trust yourself.

Cooking by the seat of your pants requires a little experience, and a willingness to do some math. Don't panic! This isn't a calculus class. But a basic understanding of ratios will take you from a so-so camp cook to an amazing camp cook. Once you know about how much water to grain you need, or water to pancake mix, as the case may be, the options are endless.

Whenever possible, we have tried to note the ratios that will help guide you in making a good meal. For example, one part oatmeal to two parts water is going to make for a very different breakfast than one part oatmeal to four parts water (hello, oatmeal soup). A good trick for mastering ratios is using your camp cup or mug to help guide you. Or just eyeball things and add ingredients slowly. Those lentils look a little dry? You don't need a cookbook to tell you to add more water. After all, cooking is basically putting common sense to good use. Don't leave home without it.

There is, however, one task that measuring is great for: meal planning. Most of the recipes in this book make two to four servings. If you're traveling with a group of eight, then it's easy to calculate how much of the base ingredients you will need to take with you.

With a little math and some creativity, you'll be on your way to being a five-star outdoor cook in no time.

—Anna

THREE-WAY
NUT BUTTER

Have you ever wanted to eat your nut butter like toothpaste? Then this recipe is for you. Inspired by all the times we've dipped into the peanut butter jar with a spoon, it's basically a homemade energy gel, except way better. After all, peanut butter, almond butter, and Nutella make the perfect trail treat trifecta.

While this Three-Way Nut Butter is great on its own, you can add various flavors to switch it up. Ground coffee pairs well with the chocolate flavor and will give you an added caffeine boost; vanilla extract will make you feel like you're eating cookie dough; honey will bring some additional sweetness.

The finished product can be stored in a plastic freezer bag and then eaten with a spoon. But if you want an easy trail treat, consider investing in a reusable squeeze tube. As the name suggests, these tubes can be refilled and provide the perfect vessel for serving this nut butter. Just squeeze and eat.

INGREDIENTS

1 part peanut butter

1 part almond butter

1 part chocolate hazelnut butter (e.g., Nutella)

FLAVORING OPTIONS

Ground coffee

Vanilla extract

Honey

PREPARATION

In a bowl, mix together the nut butters until well blended. If you would like to add an additional flavor, mix one of those in.

Place mixture in a plastic bag or reusable squeeze tube.

FISTFUL OF
MOCHA BARK

Sometimes you need a little jolt, whether it's the last mile of the day and your feet won't go any farther or the last push up the summit, because you're GOING to get that selfie. For those times there's coffee. Or rather, coffee *beans*.

Chocolate-covered coffee beans are a favorite of coffee-loving outdoorsmen and -women. Why? You don't have to take time to brew coffee, and you get a quick caffeinate fix. You can easily prep a batch of these at home before you head out on your next trip, but since individually chocolate-coated beans are time-consuming to make, we turned this into a mocha bark, letting you break off as much as you want and keep pushing forward.

Don't skimp on the quality of your coffee beans on this one; it's what's going to make or break (pun intended) the recipe. It works as well with a darker roast as it does with a lighter one, depending on your preference.

MAKES Enough for you and a couple of friends, depending on how addicted to coffee you are

INGREDIENTS

½ cup dark chocolate bar broken into small pieces

⅓ cup coffee beans

PREPARATION

Line a baking pan with parchment paper (or lay the parchment paper on a flat surface like your kitchen counter).

Melt the chocolate by placing it in a heat-proof bowl inside a saucepan with boiling water. Once the chocolate is entirely melted, stir in the coffee beans.

Use a spatula to spread the melted chocolate and coffee beans onto the parchment paper, forming an even layer.

Let cool completely then break into pieces.

Store in a sealable container or plastic freezer bag.

CHOCOLATE AND FIG
ENERGY BALLS

Most ready-to-buy energy foods can be put into the "energy glob thing" category. Whether a gel, butter, or bar, they all tend to serve the same purpose: fit in a backpack and/or pocket and be easy to eat in one bite. These energy balls do exactly that, except they're free of any weird, unpronounceable ingredients, and you can make them in big batches (if you want to). Feel free to use this as a base recipe and switch out the dried figs for other dried fruit, like chopped apricots or currants. You can also experiment with adding in a little bit of spice, like ground cinnamon or ginger. If you're heading out in very hot weather, don't be surprised if a bag of these ends up getting smashed together in your backpack. They're still going to taste delicious.

MAKES 10–14 balls

INGREDIENTS

½ cup salted peanut butter

2 tablespoons honey

3 tablespoons unsweetened cocoa powder

½ cup finely chopped figs

½ cup chocolate chips

1 cup rolled oats

PREPARATION

In a bowl, mix together the peanut butter and honey with a fork. It will have a sticky consistency, but mix together as best you can.

Add in the cocoa powder and stir together until well-blended. Add the chopped figs, chocolate chips, and rolled oats; mix.

Using your hands, mold the mixture into balls a little smaller than a walnut.

Store in an airtight container in the refrigerator (which will keep them firm).

FORK-SMASHED
HUMMUS

Hummus doesn't do so well in a cooler for an extended number of days. That's what's great about this recipe: You can make it fresh whenever you want it. All you need is a fork to do some mashing with and you're good to go. Make a batch and use it on bread for sandwiches, in a pita with falafel (page 191), or with a little flatbread cut into pieces if you're looking to have a classy camp happy hour.

MAKES About 3 to 4 servings

INGREDIENTS

1 (15-ounce) can garbanzo beans

1 to 2 cloves garlic, finely chopped

Juice of a small lemon

2 teaspoons cumin powder

¼ teaspoon salt

Dash of black pepper

PREPARATION

Open the can of garbanzo beans and strain off the liquid. You can apply Leave No Trace principles here and not only eliminate your waste, but use it to make a new dish: Save the strained liquid to add to your pasta, couscous, or falafel water.

Place the garbanzo beans in a bowl and use a fork to mash them. Mix in the rest of the ingredients until well-blended. Spread over everything in sight.

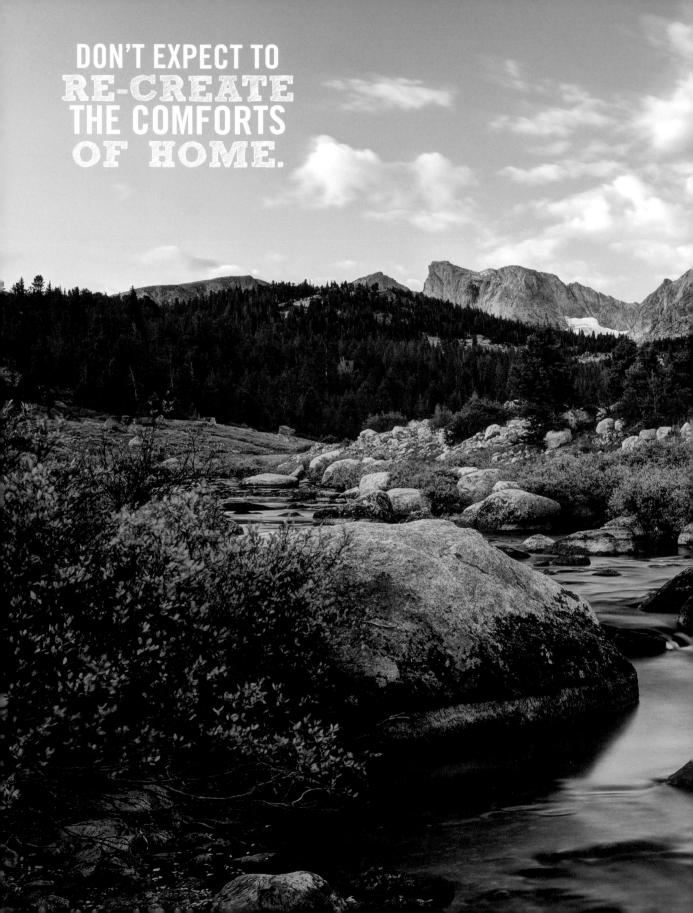

DON'T EXPECT TO RE-CREATE THE COMFORTS OF HOME.

ALPINE START
MUFFINS

For early starts you want a grab-and-go snack, and we're not talking about a stop at a fast-food restaurant for a breakfast sandwich. These muffins are made with mornings in mind. Unlike most conventional muffins, which are really just cookies disguised as something "healthy," these are dense, loaded with dried fruit and oats, and not overly sweet. You can make them with whatever dried fruit and nut combination feels right. Raisins and walnuts work well together, as do hazelnuts and figs. For early-morning starts, make these the night before, then pack them for whatever trail/beach/mountain your morning is going to take you to. Don't forget to pack the coffee thermos.

MAKES 12 large muffins

INGREDIENTS

2 eggs

⅓ cup olive oil

¼ cup honey

½ cup yogurt

½ cup milk

1 small apple, grated

1½ cups whole wheat flour

1 teaspoon baking powder

½ teaspoon baking soda

1 teaspoon ground cinnamon

¼ teaspoon salt

½ cup chopped dried fruit
(figs, raisins, currants)

½ cup chopped nuts or seeds
(walnuts, hazelnuts, sunflower seeds)

½ cup rolled oats

TOPPING

1 tablespoon honey

1 tablespoon olive oil

1 teaspoon cinnamon

½ cup rolled oats

PREPARATION

Preheat the oven to 375°F.

In a large bowl, whisk the eggs until frothy. Add the olive oil and honey and whisk together until smooth, followed by the yogurt and milk. Stir in the grated apple.

In a separate bowl, mix together the whole wheat flour, baking powder, baking soda, ground cinnamon, and salt. Add to the wet ingredients and stir together until well blended. Add the dried fruit, nuts, and rolled oats.

Spoon the batter into a muffin tin that's greased or lined with paper or silicone muffin liners.

To make the topping, mix together the honey and olive oil with a fork until fairly well blended; add the cinnamon. Mix in the oats and stir together until the oats are fully covered in the honey and olive oil blend. Sprinkle the topping over the muffin as best you can (the topping has a tendency to get very sticky) before you bake them.

Bake the muffins for 18 to 25 minutes, until a deep golden brown. Remove from the oven and let cool.

I'M GONNA GO AHEAD AND EAT THIS JUNK FOOD
ON MY VACATION

EVERY OUTDOOR ADVENTURER SHOULD HAVE A SECRET STASH OF JUNK FOOD.

Don't bother turning that package of Peanut Butter M&M's over to learn what various forms of yellow and red coloring there are, not to mention the percentage of (most likely GMO) high-fructose corn syrup that is lurking deep within those brightly-colored rounds. Don't even think about it. Grab that bag and pretend you just don't care. Dance like no one is watching, and by dance, I mean eat that junk food and enjoy every second of it.

Sure, at home you extol the values of "real food," keeping your body cleansed of the impurities imposed on us by corporate agribusiness. Out here in the wilderness? Screw it!

Let's get real: We all want a little junk food. You don't even need to go a full week before your Guilty Pleasure Cravings start kicking in. Usually they start about an hour into a trip. "I could totally go for some [insert preferred junk food item here]," you start telling yourself, or anyone who will listen.

While you might be all-kale-smoothies-all-the-time at home, pushing your body to its limits on a trip is a little different. Here you are, out on an extended backpacking trip, feet blistered to hell, shoulders sore because you should have gotten in a few more training trips in this spring but you didn't, and you need some motivation. Which is why you can go ahead and feel good about that stash of candy you have hidden somewhere. No more shame, no more hiding; come out with your sweet stash and stand proud. Say "I'm going to eat this junk food, and I am going to like it."

Because your body is going to suck up that sugar or salt or fat and put it to good use. It's going to make all those neurons in your brain explode with "Oh yeah, let's do this!" And it's going to get you across the icy river, up the peak, through the rapid.

Keep your eating strategy simple: Pack mostly healthy stuff; eat it. Pack a few indulgent things; eat those too. Don't get hung up on them—enjoy them. Food is as much about fueling yourself as it is about enjoying it. No need to get neurotic about it.

No one is going to recommend that you overdose on sugar—you won't be doing your body any favors—but a little indulgence here and there? That's just good practice. Respect yourself. Treat yourself. Have a problem with it?

Take this Oreo and keep hiking.

—Anna

TERESA'S
BALLS OF POWER

You may not think the name "Balls of Power" is as funny as my friend Teresa Bruffey and I do. That's OK. Feel free to give these things your own nickname after you make them and fall in love with them: Orbs of Energy, Super Delightful Chocolate Spheres, Semi-Healthy Sugar Bombs, whatever you want. Everyone can agree that these balls are composed of solid and necessary amounts of protein and fat, with a sweet chocolate-and-honey surprise in the middle.

MAKES 5–6 balls

INGREDIENTS

Chocolate-flavored protein powder

½ cup peanut butter (works best with no-sugar-added peanut butter such as Adams, or freshly-ground peanut butter)

Little bit of oatmeal

Honey

Chocolate chips

Soup spoon or other roundish, flattish spoon

Small plate

Plastic wrap

PREPARATION

Sprinkle ¼ cup or so of protein powder on the plate in a smooth layer. You'll be rolling sticky, gooey balls in it later, so make the area big enough for rolling. You can always add more protein powder if you run short, but it's annoying if the ball bits stick to the plate. You want a good powder coating. Set the plate aside.

In a bowl, lightly mix together a blob of peanut butter with a rough tablespoon each of protein powder and oatmeal. Don't overmix and make it too gooey. If the peanut butter is a bit on the stiff side, it will be easier to work with and will also hold up better on your adventure.

Scoop 1 tablespoon of the peanut butter–protein powder–oatmeal mixture onto your spoon. Using your finger, smoosh the mixture out to fill the space of the spoon, even allowing the mixture to extend a bit beyond the edges of the spoon. Make a depression at the center for the goodies.

Squeeze 1 teaspoon or so of honey into the depression. Then place 5 to 10 chocolate chips in and around the depression; push them down slightly so they stay in place. Use your finger to gently fold the outer edges of the peanut butter mixture toward the center to cover the chocolate chips and honey in the depression, slowly forming a ball-like shape. It's going to be sticky, and there's no perfection in power balls, so don't worry if it's not a perfect circle.

Roll the ball off the spoon and into the protein powder on the plate, being careful not to "open up" the gooey honey/chips center. Gently roll the ball around the protein powder, coating the entire surface of the ball. Wrap the ball in a small square of plastic wrap and put it in the freezer. Repeat with the remaining mixture.

Allow the balls to solidify in the freezer for at least 1 hour.

Before you head out on the trail, throw a few balls in a ziplock bag in your pack.

MILE 5
ICED COFFEE

Iced coffee: thirst quencher with a kick. A caffeinated cold drink on a hot day is almost as good as ice cream, but there's no need to wait until you get back to civilization to indulge. Got a thermos? You too can have transportable iced coffee.

This recipe is for all those outdoor coffee lovers who don't want to limit their habit to a morning activity. What's the trick to Mile 5 Iced Coffee? Coffee ice cubes. These will keep your coffee cold without diluting it so that come your afternoon coffee break, you can enjoy a swig of iced coffee that's as strong as when you brewed it.

You can make this recipe with a cold batch of brewed coffee, but we're including a recipe for an easy French press cold brew. Make the coffee and your coffee ice cubes the night before, and pour it all into a thermos the next morning. You'll be counting down to Mile 5.

Coffee Ice Cubes:
Pour brewed coffee (preferably cooled) into an ice-cube tray and put in the freezer. Once frozen, use instead of regular ice cubes to keep iced coffee cool.

French Press Cold Brew:
Because you are doing a cold extraction (as opposed to hot extraction, which is how you brew your morning coffee), you need more coffee than you usually brew with. You want to aim for a 1:7 ratio of coffee to water. This ratio is based on weight as opposed to volume, so we have done the conversion for you. For the average 34-ounce French press, this is going to be approximately:

1 cup whole coffee beans

3½ cups water

Grind the coffee beans, place them in the French press, and add cold water. Gently stir.

Cover the French press with a tea towel or tinfoil, and let it sit out overnight, ideally for 12 hours.

After the coffee has finished brewing, plunge the French press. Cold brew coffee is now ready for your thermos!

SINGLE ESPRESSO
DOUBLE CHOCOLATE COOKIES

No one has ever turned down a chocolate espresso cookie, even people who don't like coffee. Don't let the name mislead you; you won't need to pull any espresso shots to make this snack. Simply grind a few extra beans next time you're making coffee, and add them to a batch of these cookies to take on your next hike. It's like having a coffee break and a bar of chocolate, all rolled into one. Single espresso and double chocolate triples the fun.

MAKES About 24 cookies

INGREDIENTS

8 tablespoons butter, room temperature

½ cup organic cane sugar

1 egg, lightly whisked with a fork

¼ cup unsweetened cocoa powder

¾ cup all-purpose flour

3 teaspoons finely ground coffee

1 cup chocolate chips

PREPARATION

Preheat the oven to 350°F. Grease a baking sheet, or line it with a silicone baking mat.

In a large bowl, cream together the butter and sugar. Add the egg and mix together.

In a separate bowl, combine the cocoa powder, flour, ground coffee, and chocolate chips. Stir together then add to the wet ingredients. Mix together until a dough forms.

Use a tablespoon to scoop out the dough. Roll it into a ball with your hands then place it on the baking sheet, lightly pressing the top of the cookie to flatten it a little. Bake for about 15 to 20 minutes. Remove from oven and let cool completely.

Store in an airtight container.

ON THE BENEFITS OF AN EMERGENCY
CHOCOLATE STASH

THERE'S ONE THING THAT'S GOING TO GET YOU TO THE TOP OF THAT MOUNTAIN, to the campsite, or to the next mile marker. It's not tenacity or passion or commitment. Those are all good things, but out here in the wild, it's going to take a lot more than a word on that inspirational poster at the dentist's office. It's going to take chocolate.

Chocolate is going to do for you what no inspirational quote, book, or adventure partner can do. It's going to push you further than you've been before. It's going to be there when you really need it, whether it's physically or emotionally. It's going to pull you off the ground and get you going again. Chocolate isn't a trip luxury—it's an essential.

I could give you the laundry list of health benefits of chocolate—antioxidants, heart health, and all that—but you're out adventuring. You're not necessarily the target market for health tricks. Your life *is* a health trick.

But I can tell you that chocolate deserves a permanent spot on your packing list.

Just as you should always have a few $20 bills tucked away somewhere in your wallet or pack in case things get dire, the same goes for chocolate bars.

Not convinced you can push through to the summit? There's a chocolate bar for that. Feeling lonely and wondering what the hell you have gotten yourself into on this trip? Reach into that inner pocket in your backpack for a chocolate hug. Can't sleep because you're nervous about tomorrow's itinerary? Snack on that chocolate bar you stashed in your pair of clean socks. There are many things in life that lead to regret, but an emergency chocolate stash is not one of them (as long as they are appropriately packed in the event of extremely warm weather of course).

Now there's chocolate, and then there's chocolate. You think you're going to be motivated by that chalky bar that tastes more like soap than real chocolate? Sure, you saved a few bucks, but is that bar going to get you up and over the next obstacle? I doubt it. If you want motivation, you have to buy the good stuff. The stuff that makes you think: "If I can make it, I get to bite into that [insert your favorite chocolate bar here]."

A chocolate bar isn't going to do the work for you. You're still going to have to hike, climb, swim, paddle, or pedal to reach whatever milestone is the day's check-off, but chocolate is sure going to make that work a heck of a lot easier. And aren't you worth it?

—Anna

WTF DO WE DO WITH THESE
BANANAS FRITTERS?

"Mmm . . . bananas," said no one ever when looking at the dinged-up, browning bananas, moderately squished after having fallen to the bottom of the bag. A banana on Day One of a trip can be a tasty treat. Come Day Three or Four, and any still hanging around are more likely to be destined for the trash bag than your stomach. We've got a solution for that. Mix up a mashed banana with a handful of oats, and you can make simple and tasty fritters. You can serve these warm and gooey fritters for breakfast or dessert, and they're excellent when topped with a squeeze of honey.

MAKES 3–4 small fritters

INGREDIENTS

1 ripe banana

¼ cup oats

1 teaspoon cinnamon

Honey for topping

Oil for frying

PREPARATION

In a bowl, mash the banana with a fork. Add the oats and cinnamon and stir together until well blended. Let sit for 10 to 15 minutes.

Scoop out the batter with a spoon and place in a frying pan containing a little oil. Gently flatten each scoop. Fry the fritters for a couple of minutes on each side, until they are a deep golden brown.

Remove from the pan and drizzle with honey; serve immediately.

DATE HIKE—WORTHY RED
PEPPER AND OLIVE TAPENADE

Bring it in a container, spread it on a sandwich before you go, dip crackers in it, use it as a topping for pasta, eat it with a spoon—whatever you do with this tapenade, it's going to make you feel like the classiest kid on the trail. Perfect for both trail sandwiches and trail appetizers, this tapenade is sure to impress, and it won't take you long to make.

Hailing from Provence in the south of France, tapenade traditionally is a dish made with olives, capers, anchovies, and olive oil. This recipe is a little different, but it keeps the spirit of its namesake dish. The roasted red peppers bring an additional flavor that pairs well with the olives, and the almonds help make it a little chunkier (as well as giving you a little more of an energy boost). Really want to impress that date? Pair this tapenade with crackers and a little goat cheese for the ultimate trail appetizer. Or cut up a tortilla into triangles for an instant appetizer, no matter where you are. You can always add an anchovy filet or two if you would like, for some extra saltiness.

Note that this tapenade should be kept in the refrigerator, so it's not ideal for multiple-day trips; it will start to get a little funky. For a day hike, day paddle, or overnight, it will be just fine.

INGREDIENTS

1 cup roasted red peppers (about half a 16-ounce jar)

1 (6-ounce) can black olives

½ cup almonds or walnuts

1 to 2 tablespoons fresh rosemary or thyme

1 clove garlic (optional, depending on the kind of date you're on)

¼ teaspoon salt

Freshly ground black pepper

PREPARATION

Place all the ingredients in a food processor and mix until well blended. Taste, adding more salt and pepper as needed.

Store in an airtight container.

EATING
IS A JOYFUL
EXPERIENCE.

A FEW NOTES ON
DIGESTION

WHAT IS THAT SMELL IN THE TENT?

You will ask this question sometimes. The more often you ask it, rhetorically or otherwise, the unhappier you will be on your trip. Things will smell: your socks, your clothes, your sleeping bag, your tent mate's socks, your tent mate's clothes, your tent mate's sleeping bag.

There is also the threat of flatulence. Yes, this is a real thing. When you're on a backpacking trip and you spend 24 hours a day within 20 to 30 feet of someone, one or both of you may (probably will) produce and expel intestinal gases from time to time.

Here's why that happens: You're eating food you wouldn't normally eat. No matter how hard you try to eat "real food" out there, you're probably going to pack a few things that affect your digestion differently than what you eat during a normal week at home or the office. Leave kale salad at home in the refrigerator, and pack an energy bar. Eat an energy bar, read wrapper, be surprised at how much fiber it contains, furrow brow, scratch chin. Another possible scenario: Make a dehydrated backpacking meal for dinner, read outside of package, be completely alarmed at how much fiber is contained in meal, wonder if you're going to make it through the night without running to dig a hole in the ground somewhere or asphyxiating your tentmate. It happens. And it's something to think about when you're preparing your food list.

Altitude could be another factor. If you're camping or backpacking at higher altitudes than where you live, your digestion can get a little bubblier.

Another possible factor is your backpack waist belt. If you're wearing your backpack correctly, the waist belt will be pushing slightly on some of your internal organs responsible for digestion. This might affect how things move through your digestive system. Nothing to worry about.

Now, this isn't a book on etiquette, so we won't go into the proper things to do and not do regarding digestive anomalies. You can stealth things out; you can make things as loud as possible. You can crack a joke every time anyone in your group has a flatulent event; you can play the blame game. You can get angry in the night when your tent smells as though someone tossed a decomposing deer carcass into it; you can dry heave; you can refuse to sleep in the tent with a friend who has digestive issues. You can bring pills intended to remedy such things. Or you can just quietly deal with it all. Who knows? Maybe you won't have any issues.

I would offer two pieces of advice when backpacking: First, keep tabs on approximately how much fiber is in your daily diet at home, and don't go extravagantly above that when planning meals for a backcountry trip. Second, definitely give some additional thought to any sort of prepackaged meal that involves the word "chili." Just my 2 cents.

—Brendan

CANDY AISLE
ALMOND BUTTER

Nut butter is the fuel of any adventure, unless of course you're allergic to nuts. (If that's the case, we're sorry.) But like with any backcountry food staple, even the best nut butter can get downright boring by Day Three. Solution? Add chocolate. Who doesn't love a little chocolate with their lunch? If you don't, you should probably stop reading this book immediately.

There's nothing complicated about this recipe; you don't even have to use almond butter. If you don't have time to go to the candy aisle before you hit the trailhead, add broken pieces of dark chocolate instead. The point is to create a concoction that's going to make your trail mates oh so jealous. Your lunch just got a whole lot more appetizing.

MAKES Enough for a few lunches

INGREDIENTS

1 cup almond butter

½ cup any chocolate from the candy aisle

½ cup unsweetened shredded coconut

PREPARATION

Mix all the ingredients together. Spread on bread, or eat with a spoon. Rejoice in your lunch, because it's better than everyone else's.

NOTE This recipe can be adapted in a variety of ways. You can also add a handful of trail mix. Or just a handful of chocolate chips. Whatever is going to make you feel like you're getting a trail treat.

OVERNIGHT TRIPS

FIG AND ORANGE
BUCKWHEAT PORRIDGE

On cooler mornings, a hot breakfast is a welcome way to wake up. But not all hot breakfasts have to involve oatmeal. Instead of your usual bowl of oats, try a hot cereal made with buckwheat. It takes a little longer to cook than oatmeal (especially if you are used to instant), but buckwheat's nutty flavor and slightly crunchy texture are a welcome change from the usual camping breakfast routine. Don't have an orange with you? Make this with an apple. Throw in your chopped apple pieces toward the end of the cooking process so that they soften a bit.

MAKES 2 hearty portions

RATIO FOR COOKING BUCKWHEAT 1 part buckwheat groats to 2 parts water

INGREDIENTS

1 medium-size orange

2 tablespoons honey

1 cup buckwheat groats

2 cups water

¼ teaspoon salt

1 teaspoon cinnamon

½ cup chopped figs

PREPARATION

Rinse the orange and use a knife to slice off the outer part of the peel. The less pith (the white stuff) you get, the less bitter the end taste will be. Slice the pieces of peel into thin strips. Place in a pot along with the honey.

Place the pot over medium heat and let the mixture cook until the honey starts to bubble. Add the buckwheat groats, water, salt, cinnamon, and figs. Cover and bring to a boil; reduce the heat and let the buckwheat simmer about 10 to 15 minutes, until the water has cooked off. If you prefer a crunchier consistency, cook for less time; if you want it to be a little softer, cook it longer. Add more water if needed.

While the buckwheat is cooking, chop the orange into small pieces. When the buckwheat is cooked, stir in the orange pieces. Sprinkle with a little cinnamon and drizzle with honey before serving if you like.

EASY FLOUR MIX
SO YOU CAN MAKE YOUR OWN FLATBREAD WHILE CAMPING

While you probably won't be opening up a backcountry bakery busting out croissants, Danishes, and other baked treats, making flatbread over your camp stove is definitely doable. There's something comforting about making bread in the outdoors; it's warm, tastes a little smoky when singed by a hot stove, and pairs perfectly with everything from Spicy Dal with Kale (page 138) to Seven-Can Chili for Six People (page 82). Plus, you get to be that person who made fresh bread.

The only drawbacks to making flatbread on a camping trip are that it can be a bit of a pain and it's not the cleanest process. Expect to spend some time diligently washing afterward, or you'll be stuck with rock-hard dried flour on your hands and mixing bowl. If you're camping with friends and have access to two stoves, use one for the flatbreads. Otherwise, choose the order in which you want to cook your meal and flatbreads. If your main dish cooks up fairly quickly (5 minutes or less), make your flatbreads first and wrap them in a tea towel or whatever else you have on hand to keep them warm. If your main dish takes longer, like lentils, make that first, cover and set aside, then fry up your flatbread.

You can add a variety of spices to your base flatbread mix. Try a teaspoon of cumin powder or caraway seeds for a more exotic flavor, some dried basil or rosemary, or a few tablespoons of sunflower seeds for some extra crunch.

Have leftover flatbread? Wrap it up and spread it thick with peanut butter and honey the next morning.

MAKES 4–6 flatbread rounds

INGREDIENTS

½ cup all-purpose flour

½ cup whole wheat or spelt flour

1 teaspoon baking powder

¼ teaspoon salt

About ⅓ cup water

About 1 tablespoon oil, plus more for frying

PREPARATION

AT HOME In a bowl, mix together the dry ingredients. Place in a sealable bag or container. If using a bag, consider double-bagging—you do not want flour spilling all over the innards of your backpack.

AT CAMP When ready to bake, pour the flour mix into a bowl. Add about half the water to the mix and the 1 tablespoon oil. Mix together until the dough is crumbly. Add the rest of the water (more or less as needed) until the dough comes together. It should be easy to work into a ball but not runny or too sticky.

Form the dough into 4 to 6 balls, depending on the size of your pan and how big you want the flatbreads. Flatten the balls into rounds a little less than ¼ inch thick.

Fry flatbreads in a lightly oiled pan for about 2 to 3 minutes on each side, depending on thickness. Dark brown spots will form on the flatbread as it cooks. Be careful not to let it burn.

CAR CAMP
CHILAQUILES

If you need convincing to cook and eat a dish that basically translates to "breakfast nachos," I can't help you. Sorry.

Car Camp *Chilaquiles* is a campground version of the Mexican breakfast dish (although some people might say it's closer to Tex-Mex *migas*) that you can cook with basic ingredients. Whatever you call it, it's a big breakfast that won't leave you dragging a mile up the hiking trail.

It's a bit more involved than making instant oatmeal or granola, but worth some extra prep time. Get one of your friends to help you prep—give him or her a job slicing veggies or cheese, or cracking eggs, and this will go a lot faster.

You're going to need at least one 10-inch frying pan with a lid. Two frying pans make it easier but are not mandatory. Use whatever tortilla chips you prefer for this dish; I like basic corn chip strips like Fritos.

MAKES Enough for 3–4 people who whine about being hungry in the morning

INGREDIENTS

4 ounces Monterey Jack cheese

½ yellow onion

½ red bell pepper

2 ounces olive oil

6 eggs

1 (4-ounce) bag corn chips

1 (4.5-ounce) can mild chopped green chiles

1 (4.5-ounce) can hot chopped green chiles

1 16-ounce jar salsa

Hot sauce (optional)

MEAT OPTIONAL

NOTE You can easily halve this recipe if you're cooking for fewer people, or if you don't own an enormous frying pan.

PREPARATION

Slice cheese into thin sections.

Slice onions and pepper and sauté in the oil in a 10-inch frying pan over medium heat. Remove from heat (move veggies to a separate plate while you cook the eggs).

Crack eggs, scramble in frying pan, and cook until almost dry. Remove from heat and add to peppers and onions.

Arrange corn chips in a layer on your pan until the bottom is covered evenly.

Pour scrambled eggs, peppers, and onions on top of corn chips.

Spread mild green chiles and hot green chiles evenly over the top of the eggs, peppers, and onions.

Arrange the cheese slices on top of the eggs and vegetables. Place the lid over the frying pan and cook over low heat until cheese is melted.

Cut a panful of *chilaquiles* into four equal triangular sections.

Try, and fail, to gracefully serve the *chilaquiles* with layers intact. Give up and just heave approximately one-fourth of the entire dish onto each person's plate or bowl. Add salsa and/or hot sauce as desired.

Eat, wash dishes, and then do something that burns a lot of calories.

YES, I'M GOING TO
BREW A CUP OF COFFEE
FOR LUNCH, AND IF YOU DON'T WANT
TO WAIT FOR ME YOU CAN GO
AHEAD WITHOUT ME

LOOK, EVERYONE HAS NEEDS. Some people feel they deserve a parking lot beer to relax after their hike. I am going to drink coffee midday. Sometimes I do this with a canned iced-coffee drink; other times I pack an entire Jetboil stove and fuel canister just to boil water somewhere. Often on a backpacking trip, I'll leave my stove near the top of my pack so I can easily access it after lunch.

I understand that this might throw you for a bit of a loop; we're out here to hike, not sit around and casually drink coffee. But what's more wonderful than polishing off a nice hiking lunch on a summit of a mountain or sitting next to an alpine lake and washing it down with a strong cup of hot coffee? Yes, I realize people are walking by, and maybe they're saying, "Look at these idiots brewing a cup of coffee up here—how ridiculous." Maybe they're saying that because it's windy up here, or raining, or sleeting. That's possible. It's also possible that they're total amateurs at this hiking thing and don't have their act together enough to orchestrate the process of making a cup of coffee out here.

If you don't feel like you can wait that long, I'll tell you what: Head down the trail, and my properly caffeinated self will catch you in a few minutes. Coffee is good for all sorts of things, like cancer prevention, mental focus, digestive health, and athletic endurance. So today, it's actually a performance-enhancing supplement.

You might argue that a stove and fuel weigh too much to carry in a day pack. Well, the stove and fuel weigh a total of 1 pound. You might say that when we're hiking, we don't have time to stop and brew coffee. The whole process, including my drinking said cup of coffee, will only take about 15 minutes. You might say, hey, coffee is a diuretic and will dehydrate you at high altitudes. I can't argue with that, because you're right.

I'm not arguing with you, or trying to persuade you to wait for me while I make coffee here on the side of the trail. You're free to think what you want, even if that means you think I'm an idiot for hauling all this stuff up here to brew a single cup of coffee. I wouldn't say I'm civilized, but I certainly have enough sense to know when it's appropriate to drink coffee, which is any time I *want* to drink coffee.

Oh, did you want some coffee too? Great! Because I brought enough for both of us.

—*Brendan*

SEVEN-CAN CHILI
FOR SIX PEOPLE

This chili is no joke. It really is for six people—maybe for seven. And if you don't have that many friends, you'll make some at the campsite. This is an easy outdoor meal that doesn't take a whole lot of thought, and it's perfect if you are on a trip like a bike tour where you are restocking regularly! Crack open a few cans and get cooking.

Don't have five friends to share this with? You can decrease the recipe as you see fit; just keep the tomato to "other stuff" ratio about the same. The onion and garlic are optional if you need to keep this a "strictly cans" recipe, but if you have them on hand, they add a little extra flavor.

MAKES About 6 servings

INGREDIENTS

2 tablespoons olive oil

2 teaspoons cumin powder

2 teaspoons chipotle powder

3 (15-ounce) cans diced tomatoes

1 (15-ounce) can kidney beans, drained

1 (15-ounce) can black beans, drained

1 (15-ounce) can corn, drained

1 (4-ounce) can diced green chiles

OPTIONAL

3 cloves garlic, finely chopped

1 small onion, finely chopped

MEAT OPTIONAL

PREPARATION

If you are cooking with the optional onion and garlic, add these to a pot with the olive oil, cumin powder, and chipotle powder. Cook over medium heat until the onions have started to turn translucent.

Add the cans of tomatoes, beans, corn and chiles. (If you are not cooking with onion and garlic, add in the spices with the tomatoes and beans.)

Bring the chili to a simmer and cook for about 5 minutes, or as long as you can wait before you go hungry; cooking it a little longer lets the flavor develop more. Keep the chili on low heat and stir occasionally while cooking so that it doesn't stick to the bottom of the pan.

Remove from the stove and spoon into bowls to serve.

KNIFE, FORK, SPORK, OR SPOON?
A BACKCOUNTRY DILEMMA, SOLVED (IN MY OPINION)

WHEN YOU'RE IN AN OUTDOOR GEAR STORE, YOU MAY FEEL A BIT OF "CHOICE PARALYSIS" in the eating utensils aisle: Should you get a plastic spoon or a plastic fork? Both? A titanium spork? An interlocking steel knife-fork-spoon set? A spoon that folds into a coffee cup that nests inside a bowl that nests inside a cooking pot? Titanium chopsticks?

Keep it simple. Keep it light. Keep it absolutely functional. And remember the Antoine de Saint-Exupery quote: "Perfection is achieved, not when there is nothing more to add, but when there is nothing left to take away."

After years of rigorous, exhaustively documented testing in both the backcountry and the frontcountry, I feel confident that the spoon is the most superior eating utensil ever created. Yes, you've probably read a similarly superlative statement in a review of a base layer top or a pair of socks, so let's give this some thought.

Check it out: The spoon is a tiny shovel for your face. After a blizzard, when you want to get dozens of cubic feet of snow off your driveway, do you go out there with a pitchfork, a pair of broomsticks, or a shovel? That's right. The spoon is the most efficient method of moving food into your mouth in the backcountry. After a long day of hiking, you want to get food into your digestive system, preferably quickly. You use a spoon.

Oh, you use a spork? I mean, to each his or her own. But don't you think the spork is kind of the futon of the eating utensil world? It tries to be two things at once, and does both jobs pretty poorly. Unless you're talking about the type of spork that is a fork on one end and a spoon on the other—those work better but still have fork problems. Like when you accidentally break a tine off the fork, thereby decreasing its carrying capacity by 25 percent. That blows. It's pretty hard to break a spoon.

Maybe you have a titanium spork or fork-and-spoon set. It's your money. But have you ever, before a trip, realized you don't know where your special camping eating utensil is and frantically searched your house for it? You own lots of spoons. Calm down and grab one out of the kitchen drawer. It probably only weighs a few grams more than the missing one anyway.

I think it's safe to say that the spoon did for eating what the camming unit did for traditional rock climbing. Before spoons we ate with our hands, which was messy, especially when you got spaghetti sauce in your cuticles. Human beings improve the smartphone every few months, but the spoon has been the same for thousands of years. That's perfection.

"But I can't eat noodles with a spoon," you say. Yes, you can. Have you ever put an 8-foot-long tree branch in a campfire? You broke it into two to four pieces first. Do that with your fettuccine or udon before cooking it, and our friend the spoon will have no problem moving it from your bowl to your mouth. Or pack something easier to fit into a camping pot, like fusilli, elbow macaroni, penne, rice, couscous. . . . You get the idea.

Do you want to spread peanut butter on a tortilla? Your spoon works as a butter knife. It handles soup with ease, and in a pinch can be used to move water out of shallow desert potholes into your water bottle. Your spoon will never turn against you. Respect your spoon, appreciate it, and it will fill you up and never let you down.

—*Brendan*

ERIK'S CANYONLANDS
WHITE BEAN CHILI

This book has two chili recipes. "Two chili recipes?" you ask. That's right. "Why?" Because I thought all chili was the same until my friend Erik Wardell brought this white bean chili out to our annual gathering at Canyonlands National Park in 2014 and blew my mind. I have since made this recipe almost a dozen times. I think you will find it similarly addicting for two reasons:

> It is a wonderfully flavorful and unique chili recipe.

> It is easy to make. Seriously, you have to cut two things: garlic and an onion. If you can handle measuring some spices and opening five cans, you can handle this recipe and wow your friends.

I recommend making this at home a night or two before your car camping trip. Put it in a sealed container and rewarm it when you get to the campground. I think chili tastes better after it's had a day or two to marinate, and I think you'll agree that this is more flavorful rewarmed than it is straight off the stovetop. But do whatever you like.

MAKES 4–6 good-size bowls

INGREDIENTS

1 tablespoon olive oil

1 medium white or gold onion, chopped

3 cloves garlic, chopped

2 (16-ounce) cans cannellini or great northern beans

1 (16-ounce) can hominy

2–3 cups water

4 vegetable bouillon cubes

1 teaspoon ground cumin

1 teaspoon dried oregano

½ teaspoon black pepper

¼ teaspoon cayenne pepper

½ teaspoon garlic powder

2 (4-ounce) cans chopped green chiles

1 bunch cilantro, chopped

MEAT OPTIONAL

OPTIONAL

½ cup heavy whipping cream

Sour cream

Cheese

PREPARATION

Pour olive oil into a soup pot and sauté onions and garlic.

Add beans, hominy, water, veggie bouillon cubes, spices, and green chiles. Bring to a boil; reduce heat to low and simmer for 30 minutes.

Add fresh cilantro and (optional) whipping cream just before serving. Top with whipping cream, sour cream, or cheese if desired.

NOTE This recipe still tastes great if you only make half. If you do, stick with the full can of hominy, because who's going to use up half a can of hominy?

FRYING PAN
FRENCH TOAST

You don't need a skillet to make this, but it's going to look a whole lot better if you use one. And isn't looking good what we're all after in the outdoors? All jokes aside, regardless of your cooking setup, french toast is certainly going to make you look like a cook who knows what he or she is doing. Bonus points if you serve these to campers who are still in their sleeping bags.

This recipe is great for putting a few broken pieces of bread to good use, or making sure the leftover end bits in the bag don't go to waste. Top the french toast with honey or a few spoonfuls of Backpacker's Fruit Compote (page 174).

MAKES 3–4 servings

INGREDIENTS

4 eggs

2 tablespoons honey

1 teaspoon ground cinnamon

1 teaspoon ground ginger

6–8 medium-size bread slices

Oil for frying pan

PREPARATION

In a bowl, whisk the eggs with a fork until frothy. Add the honey, cinnamon, and ginger and whisk together until well blended.

Soak your bread slices in the egg mixture. Depending on the size of your bowl, you may need to do this in two rounds, soaking the first batch then adding the second once you have started cooking the first.

Place a frying pan over medium heat and grease with a little oil. Fry soaked bread slices until browned on both sides. Remove from the pan as they are done.

Top with honey or fruit compote (optional). Serve and enjoy!

DIY PANCAKES
WITH M&M'S

Stepping up your outdoor cooking game should not only be fun (and delicious), it should also be Broke-Backpacker-Friendly. When you don't have to spend money on premade meals and packaged mixes, you can invest that money in the fancy tent you've been drooling over instead. Pancake mix is a perfect example of something you can skip at the grocery store. Flour, sugar, and baking powder are all you need to make your own pancake mix. Once you master this recipe, your days of overly sweet, far-too-many-preservative pancakes will be a mere memory. You can breeze past the aisle of pancake mixes and take a moment of silence for those poor souls who don't know any better.

Before you make the batter for these pancakes, you should play around with the base mix recipe. Add additional spices like cardamom or ginger for some extra flavor. Throw in a handful of nuts or seeds if you're feeling wild.

You can increase or decrease the base recipe depending on how many servings of pancakes you are going to need on your trip. When the time comes to make breakfast, all you have to do is add water. Don't worry about measuring; just add water slowly until the consistency is a little thick and drippy, like melted ice cream.

MAKES 6–8 medium pancakes

INGREDIENTS

1 cup flour

1 tablespoon baking powder

1 tablespoon organic cane sugar

1 teaspoon cinnamon

¼ teaspoon salt

Oil for frying pan

BRING TO CAMPSITE

M&M's

PREPARATION

AT HOME Mix all the dry ingredients together and store in a lightweight sealable container or plastic bag.

AT CAMP To turn the mix into batter, add about 1 part pancake mix to 1 part water. Go slowly so that you get the right consistency; it's easier to add a little more water than it is to add more dry mix. Stir together until smooth.

Place a frying pan over medium heat, with a little oil if needed. Drop a spoonful of batter onto the frying pan. Press a few (or a ton of) M&M's into the batter. Once the pancake is firm around the edges and bubbles pop in the middle, flip it over and cook until done.

Serve immediately, or let the pancake cool and store it in your pocket for Pocket Pancakes somewhere down the trail.

REMEMBER—
COFFEE-MAKING IS
**ALL ABOUT
THE BEANS.**

AN EXHAUSTIVE BREAKDOWN OF BACKCOUNTRY
COFFEE-MAKING METHODS

IF YOU THINK INSTANT COFFEE IS THE BE-ALL AND END-ALL OF OUTDOOR COFFEE BREWING, you can stop reading right this very second. We probably can't be friends. If you believe that coffee brewing outdoors deserves some thought and care, read on.

Instant coffee has its place, and these days instant coffee is not synonymous with bad taste. Considering that today there are brands of specialty instant coffee, even the laziest of outdoor enthusiasts can brew a tasty morning cup.

But you, my friend, are not lazy. If you were, you wouldn't have picked up a book about cooking in the outdoors. You are an individual who wants more out of your meals. You are a connoisseur of the finer things, a lover of puffy jackets and delicious pilafs. You care about your chocolate bars ("single origin, minimum 60 percent cacao please"). You want other people to look at you and say, "That guy/girl is doing life right." You want rugged finesse and outdoor class. You can get it all with your coffee.

Which brew method is right for you? There's no right answer; it all depends on your coffee wants and needs. More of an espresso lover? Moka pot or Aeropress might be your jam. Big cups of filter coffee? A pour-over setup might be better suited to you.

Whatever coffee-making methods you're using, remember this: It's all about the beans. No matter how much of a brewmaster you might be, you can't magically turn cheap beans into an excellent cup. Sure, that fantastic view will help a mediocre cup taste better than it would at home, but if you start off with a bad product, you can't expect a tasty result. So don't skimp; bring the beans you would want to be drinking at home.

As for those beans, if you're coffee-obsessed, you may choose to travel with a small hand grinder. There are plenty of options to choose from, including popular Japanese brands like Porlex and Hario. If you don't want to travel with a grinder, grind your beans at home, store them in an airtight container, and try to keep them away from too much heat. In other words, don't place them in a plastic bag strapped to the top of your backpack during the height of summer.

Now, let's discuss brew methods.

French Press

Perhaps the most classic of big-batch coffee brewing methods, a French Press is ideal if you're making coffee for a large group in a base camp setting. Most traditional French presses, made out of glass, are not the kind of thing you want to be lugging along in your backpack. But for a car camping scenario, they're great. You can also buy more camp-friendly units that are insulated and more durable; titanium or stainless steel French presses are a little more rugged and lightweight.

Pour-over

If weight is a concern and you're only planning to make one or two cups of coffee at a time, a pour-over setup is probably your best option. The traditional pour-over setup—which is usually cone shaped and sits on top of your coffee cup—requires a filter, either paper or a reusable fabric one. Other pour-over setups are entirely reusable, with the filter system built in and placed either in your cup or on top of. Paper filters can make coffee cleanup easy—all you need to do is remove the filter full of grounds and place it in your trash bag—but a reusable filter will work every time, no extra accessories required.

Moka pot/Bialetti

For the espresso-loving crowd, a Moka pot is a must. These stovetop espresso makers brew a strong coffee, similar in taste to espresso. One drawback is that they are heavy, so not ideal for trips where weight is a concern. You also will want to make sure you have the correct size, depending on how many people you want to brew coffee for. Brewing batch after batch can prove difficult, as the base of the Moka pot is extremely hot directly after brewing. It needs to sit and cool down before it can be picked up and used to brew another batch.

Aeropress

Because of its size, weight, and simplicity, it's no surprise that the Aeropress (made by the same people that created the Aerobie disc that an adventurer or two has probably taken along on a trip) is popular among traveling coffee lovers. It's perfect if you're making coffee for one or two people, but you wouldn't want to use it to serve coffee to a crowd, unless you really like pressing coffee again and again.

Percolator

Percolators are reminiscent of days gone by: Scout camp trips and brightly colored enamelware of the 1970s. A percolator can sit on your camp stove or over a fire to brew coffee. Coffee purists would say that percolators have a tendency to over-extract the coffee, meaning you are left with a bitter, burnt taste that often requires milk to hide.

Cowboy coffee

Another iconic method of coffee brewing from the good old cowboy days is still used in today's cowboy community. The idea is simple: Add grounds and water to a kettle, bring to a rolling boil, serve. There are variations on this method; for example, pouring in a little cold water right afterward, which helps the grounds sink and stops the extraction process, making the coffee taste better. You can also bring water to a boil, add grounds, let it steep for 5 minutes, then serve. While cowboy coffee has a reputation for being full of grounds, if you pour carefully, you should be able to get a cup of coffee with only a few straggling grounds in it.

Straight coffee beans

Screw the brew and skip right to the beans. Chewing on whole coffee beans can be an instant pick-me-up and doesn't require any work at all. And if that doesn't sound appetizing, consider enjoying them covered in chocolate, like a Fistful of Mocha Bark (page 42).

—Anna

CHEDDAR AND MUSTARD
FLATBREAD QUESADILLA

Travel to any country where cheese is in abundance, and chances are you will come across some interpretation of "two layers of starch with melted cheese inside." But that's a mouthful, so we're sticking with the word most of us know: quesadilla. Unlike a normal quesadilla, however, this one is made with flatbread. It's the kind of appetizer you could serve up on a trip where you're trying to impress someone and prove that you're marriage material. Or that you're not marriage material because you're not interested in the normal confines of traditionally defined unions, but you do want to show that you're partner material and that you're a hell of a cook. Whatever your reasons, grill up a few of these and you'll be well on your way to outdoor cooking stardom.

MAKES 1 quesadilla

INGREDIENTS

1–3 tablespoons mustard (depending on spiciness)

2 pieces flatbread

Medium or sharp cheddar

4–6 thin slices red pepper

PREPARATION

Spread a thin layer of mustard on both pieces of flatbread. Cut thin slices of cheese and place on top of the mustard layer on one of the pieces of flatbread. Evenly arrange the slices of red pepper. Cover with a few more slices of cheese, and place the second piece of flatbread on top, mustard side down.

In a frying pan, grill the flatbread on medium heat until the cheese starts to melt, regularly flipping so that you don't burn the bread.

Remove from frying pan and cut into fourths. Serve immediately. Revel in how classy you seem compared to that guy at the other campsite who's just eating a bag of chips.

POOR CAMPER'S
PANINI TWO WAYS

"Grilled cheese sandwich" sounds like you are eating in an elementary school cafeteria; "panini" sounds like you're trying to impress someone. In terms of Easy Recipes That Sound Fancy, this is one of the easiest. All you need are some bread slices (although something other than your everyday sandwich bread is nice if you want to switch it up) and cheese. You can spice up the panini depending on what you're in the mood for and what you've got stocked in the cooler. Here we've got two of our favorite versions—one that's a little sweeter and one that's a little spicier. It's up to you to decide how you want the evening to go.

Poor Camper's Panini with Mustard and Apples

MAKES 2 servings

INGREDIENTS

4 pieces bread of your choice

A few slices of sharp cheddar

1 small apple, thinly sliced

Mustard

PREPARATION

Make your sandwiches. For best results, make sure there is a layer of cheese, then another ingredient, then another layer of cheese. Place in a frying pan and cook until cheese is melted. Serve.

Poor Camper's Panini with Jalapeños

MAKES 2 servings

INGREDIENTS

4 pieces bread of your choice

A few slices of sharp cheddar

1 (4-ounce) can diced jalapeños

PREPARATION

Make your sandwiches. For best results, make sure there is a layer of cheese, then another ingredient, then another layer of cheese. Place in a frying pan and cook until cheese is melted. Serve.

MEAT OPTIONAL

THE MORE YOU KNOW, THE LESS YOU NEED
SPICE KIT

A spice kit is an essential part of a proper camp kitchen. But a spice kit doesn't need to be complicated. In fact, with just a few key spices, you can revolutionize any meal.

What's included in your spice kit is up to you. You may find that over time you add or remove certain spices depending on what you're cooking or how long a trip you are going on and how lightweight you are attempting to travel. But one thing is certain: Do not leave home without a spice kit. If you do, your meals will be bland and boring, and you'll be one of those people who complain about how bad the food is when you go camping.

—Anna

WHAT SHOULD YOU STORE YOUR SPICES IN?

Film canisters used to be perfect as spice containers, but that's going to date you (and if you're not careful, the lids can pop off). Small, lightweight but durable containers with a screw-on lid are what you're looking for. They pack easily, and the screw-on lid gives you the peace of mind of knowing that you're not going to open your bag to find a cinnamon and olive oil explosion.

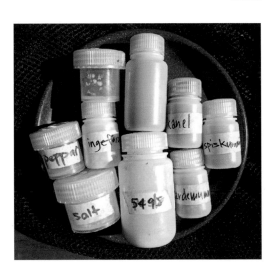

WHAT SPICES SHOULD YOU PACK?

Here is a list of the most common spices used in this book:

DRY	LIQUID
Salt	Olive oil
Ground black pepper	Soy sauce
Ground cinnamon	**OTHER SPICES THAT COULD BE GAME CHANGERS FOR YOUR OUTDOOR COOKING ROUTINE**
Ground ginger	
Chili powder (opt for chipotle if you like a smokier flavor)	Cardamom (excellent in oatmeal)
	Red pepper flakes (for when you don't have hot sauce)
Cumin powder	Coriander seeds (gives anything a slightly exotic taste)

SKIP THE FAMILY REUNION AND
GO CAMPING PASTA SALAD

Pasta salad might have a reputation as the dish you make before heading to Aunt Susan's house for the annual family get-together, but there's no reason it should be reserved for picnics and awkward family affairs. At the campground table, your uncle won't ask you if you have a real job yet, and you won't have to eat any of those nasty hot dogs just to be polite, but you can enjoy a big bowl of pasta salad. The real benefit of making pasta salad at camp? It is easy to make in large quantities, which is helpful if you're camping with a group, and it doesn't need to be served at any specific temperature. So you can make it, put it aside while you do your other camp tasks, and come back to it whenever you like.

MAKES 4 servings

INGREDIENTS

4 servings any small pasta
(penne, elbows, farfalle, etc)

1 medium apple, cored and chopped

1 red pepper, sliced

8-ounce square of feta cheese

3 tablespoons olive oil

2 tablespoons honey

1–2 tablespoons mustard

Fresh or dried basil

PREPARATION

Cook your pasta until al dente. Strain the water, and add the chopped apple and red pepper. Break the feta into the salad in small pieces, or cut it with a knife.

To make the dressing, pour the olive oil, honey, and mustard into a bowl. Whisk together with a fork. Pour the dressing over the pasta salad, add a handful of fresh basil leaves (or a couple tablespoons dried basil leaves), and mix the whole salad together. Serve at your preferred temperature.

CAMPFIRE
CORN ON THE COB

Corn is one of the easiest things to cook on a camping trip, mostly because you don't really need to do anything to it. All you need is a campfire. Some people simply cook their corn in the husk. But we find it a little easier to wrap the unhusked ears in tinfoil to prevent burning and overcooking the corn. This also ensures that you trap the steam created from the heat and helps cook the corn thoroughly and evenly

Some recipes recommend that you soak the corn in water before cooking. This is pretty much as simple as it gets: Wrap corn in tinfoil, place in fire, eat.

INGREDIENTS

As many ears of corn as you want

Tinfoil to cover the ears of corn

PREPARATION

Get a campfire going. Do this with ample time before you think you're going to be hungry, because you'll want some coals, not flames, to cook the corn.

Wrap the corn in tinfoil and place it in the coals. Cover the ears of corn with more coals.

Let the corn roast for 10 to 20 minutes. Cooking time depends entirely on the intensity of your fire and coals.

Find some sticks and maneuver the ears of corn out of the fire without burning yourself. Trust us: You do not want to remove these with your hands.

Once the corn has had a little time to cool, unwrap the tinfoil and pull back the husks. Eat as is, spread on some butter, or drizzle with olive oil and then sprinkle with salt.

AFTERMARKET MODIFICATIONS
FOR DEHYDRATED AND FREEZE-DRIED MEALS

THE DEHYDRATED AND FREEZE-DRIED MEAL GAME HAS EVOLVED OVER THE YEARS. We are no longer subject to the horror of meals that barely resemble meals and taste like something that was halfway cooked and then put in the blender. Thanks to brands like Good To-Go, Patagonia Provisions, and AlpineAire, dehydrated meals ain't what they used to be. But despite the quality of dehydrated meals straight out of the bag, there's no reason you can't get creative with them.

You could stick to the dehydrated meal as is, but if you're in need of a little something else, it's time to consider aftermarket modifications. Aftermarket modifications are really anything that you want to do to boost the flavor of your meal, from adding other ingredients to doubling up on spices. Here are a few of our favorite ways to bring some additional flavor to any dehydrated meal.

Use a dehydrated meal as a base for something else

There are no instant meal police out there; if you want to use your meal as a base for something else, go for it. Turn a soup into a pasta sauce, or make an extra side of couscous.

Spice, spice, spice

Some instant meals have a reputation for being a bit bland. Thankfully, that's starting to change, but it certainly shouldn't stop you from getting creative with how you use your own spices. Soy sauce, red chile pepper flakes, cumin powder, and cinnamon can all bring additional flavor to a meal. If it's not spice you're after, a super simple addition like a drizzle of olive oil can help give the dish a little more life.

Add some texture

Nuts, dried fruit, and grains are an easy way to add some additional texture (and flavor) to a meal without having to work very hard. Extra peanuts in a pad thai, raisins in a curry, and couscous in a chili are all simple ways to put a spin on an easy-to-make meal.

Add a little bit of fresh ingredients

Easy fresh ingredients, like chopped garlic or onion, can make an instant meal feel a little less instant.

Don't forget the hot sauce

Honestly, did you really need that hint?

—Anna

ORANGE AND RAISIN COUSCOUS
FOR SCURVY PREVENTION
(EVEN THOUGH THAT'S NOT REALLY A THING ANYMORE)

OK, so scurvy isn't a health concern anymore, but bringing an orange on a trip can add some much-needed freshness to your palate. The sweetness of the orange and the dried raisins gives this savory dish a nice balance. And since it involves couscous, it cooks up almost faster than you can say Orange and Raisin Couscous for Scurvy Prevention (Even though That's Not Really a Thing Anymore).

MAKES 2 servings

RATIO FOR COOKING COUSCOUS About 3 parts couscous to 4 parts water

INGREDIENTS

¾ cup couscous

½ cup raisins

1 teaspoons cumin powder

1 small onion, chopped

½ cup pine nuts

1 cup water

1 orange, peeled and chopped

Salt

Pepper

Olive oil

PREPARATION

In a bowl, combine the dry couscous, raisins, cumin powder, onion, and pine nuts; mix together.

Bring the water to a boil and pour over the couscous. Cover and let sit for about 5 minutes. Uncover and fluff.

Stir in the chopped orange, along with any orange juice that's leftover on your cutting board.

Sprinkle with salt and pepper, and drizzle with olive oil before serving.

CLEAN OUT THE COOLER
VEGETABLE SAUTÉ

The days of your trip are waning, and your cooler is filled with remnants of your good culinary intentions that now seem a distant memory: a piece of broccoli that's starting to yellow; half an onion that's on the verge of drying out; that impulse zucchini you grabbed at the grocery store on the way out of town because you thought "This time I'll eat more greens!" Don't you dare throw any of those out! Vegetable sautés are the outdoor enthusiast's answer to waste-free cooking and getting a healthy meal. In all honesty, you don't really need a recipe for this. You know exactly what to do: Chop up all your leftover vegetables, throw them in a pan or a pot with some oil, sauté, and call it a day.

The trick with a good vegetable sauté—and a vegetable sauté where you're trying to revive some half-dead vegetables—is garlic. So always make sure you save a clove or two for the end of a trip. You just never know. While your vegetable selection may differ, here's a vegetable sauté that's easy to prepare in case you need some guidance (or inspiration).

MAKES 2–3 servings

INGREDIENTS

2–3 tablespoons olive oil

1–2 cloves garlic, finely chopped

1 medium-size onion, finely chopped

1 teaspoon cumin powder

1 large carrot, sliced into rounds

1 stalk broccoli, chopped

1 large zucchini, sliced into rounds

Salt and pepper to taste

PREPARATION

In a pan or pot, heat the olive oil, chopped garlic, chopped onion, and cumin powder. Let sizzle for a few minutes until the onion pieces turn translucent. Add the carrot, broccoli, and zucchini and sauté until vegetables have softened a little, 5 to 10 minutes.

Serve with salt, pepper, and whatever other assortment of spices you have in your spice kit.

OPTIONAL Make Three-Ingredient (besides Peanuts) Peanut Sauce (page 144) to serve on top.

MEAT OPTIONAL

THERE'S CLEAN, AND THERE'S "CLEAN ENOUGH": A WORD ABOUT BACKCOUNTRY DISHWASHING

AT WYOMING'S CIRQUE OF THE TOWERS, I WATCHED THE SKY SLOWLY TURN BLACK over the jagged granite peaks rising hundreds of feet above the valley below. As I stood in the fading daylight, I scrubbed our cooking pot with nothing but my finger and some cold water we'd filtered out of Lonesome Lake a couple hours earlier.

If you inspected our pot under fluorescent lights, you'd probably discover remnants of the following: six mornings of oatmeal with powdered peanut butter and dried fruit and six dinners ranging from Asian noodles with peanut sauce to couscous to pesto pasta. Not a drop of soap had graced the inside of the pot since before we started our seven-day backpacking trip. We hadn't washed our dishes or flatware in hot sudsy water or run them through a heated drying cycle in a dishwasher. We hadn't worried the slightest about getting all the fragments of last night's dinner out of the pot so it would be clean for our oatmeal the next morning.

There are certain things you compromise on if you want to watch sunrises in the backcountry, and a level of cleanliness is one of them. You will go a few days without bathing or a shower; you will end up getting dirt on your clothes (and sometimes in your food); and you won't be able to get your dishes clean enough to put them back in your cupboard when you get home from your trip.

I've heard one of the best ways to make yourself miserable when traveling is to expect to re-create all the comforts of home wherever you go, rather than relaxing and accepting your new environment as it is and adjusting your expectations accordingly.

Obviously you can take a bottle of biodegradable soap and a little sponge with you in the backcountry, but if you're backpacking, that's more weight in your pack. It also requires you to use more filtered water to rinse your dishes. Don't do it in a creek or lake, because you're both polluting the water and rinsing your dishes with untreated water.

The simplest method of dishwashing is to pour some filtered water in your dishes and scrub with your finger. Yes, it takes a while, but when you're on a backpacking trip, you don't have a lot of other stuff on your schedule, do you?

For extra efficiency, weight savings, and "Roughing It" points, use the same mug or bowl for everything—eating meals and drinking coffee in the morning. This makes for fewer dishes to do, as well as a unique satisfaction from the simplicity of life in the backcountry.

For even more Roughing It points, drink the dishwater instead of scattering it into the woods near your camp kitchen. Is it gross? I mean, it's just water flavored like whatever you just ate for dinner or breakfast. I don't like to call anyone soft or anything, but if you can handle sleeping on the ground and pooping in a hole in the dirt, you can probably handle a little dishwater.

Yes, there might be a few pieces of pasta or oats, or traces of sauce around your dishes—that's OK. Back in civilization, "clean" is objective; something is either clean or it's not. When you're cooking in the backcountry, "clean enough" is in the eye of the beholder. You're eating oatmeal out of that pan, not sterilizing surgical instruments in it.

—*Brendan*

TIPS FOR MAKING GRANOLA

> Mix your oil and sweetener together before adding to the dry mix. If you are using a thicker sweetener, like honey, warming the honey and oil on the stove can make it easier to mix them together.

> Add dried fruit *after* you have baked the granola. This keeps the fruit from drying out.

> Want granola with more clusters? Whip an egg white and add it to the mixture.

> Chocolate fiend? Mix in some chocolate chips or chopped dark chocolate after the granola has baked and cooled.

MAKING YOUR OWN GRANOLA ISN'T ROCKET SCIENCE
GRANOLA

Granola is essentially oats plus some dried fruit, nuts or seeds, and spices, all mixed together with a little sweetener and then baked. It's really no more complex than that, and to prepare good granola at home before your trip, you're only limited by your creativity.

To begin with, you want to aim for somewhere in the range of 6 to 8 parts dry ingredients to 1 part wet. Of that wet ingredient, you want a little less than half to be a sweetener (like honey or maple syrup) and a little more than half to be an oil (like olive oil or coconut). If you like a sweeter granola, you can change that ratio. You can veer from this basic ratio a bit and experiment as you get more used to making granola.

For some direction, we've come up with a table of ideas for fun combinations. Of course nothing is stopping you from mixing and matching a variety of nuts, fruits, and spices in your granola. Again, not rocket science, just plain old food.

NUTS /SEEDS	DRIED FRUIT	SPICE	OTHER
Hazelnuts	Apricots	Fennel	Rye Flakes
Almonds	Cranberries	Orange Zest	Puffed Rice
Walnuts	Figs	Ginger	Coconut Flakes
Pumpkin Seeds	Raisins	Nutmeg	Flax Seeds
Pecans	Cherries	Cardamom	Shredded Coconut

INGREDIENTS

3 cups rolled oats

1 cup nuts or seeds

1 cup shredded coconut

3–4 teaspoons various spices

1 teaspoon salt

⅔ cup oil

⅓ cup honey

1 cup dried fruit, finely chopped

PREPARATION

Preheat the oven to 325°F.

Combine the dry ingredients and spices, except for the dried fruit, in a bowl.

In a separate bowl, whisk together the oil and honey and pour over the dry ingredients. Stir together until the dry ingredients are fully coated.

Spread the granola out evenly on a baking sheet and bake for 20 to 30 minutes, stirring the mixture every 10 minutes.

Remove the granola from the oven and let it cool before adding dried fruit or chocolate.

Store in an airtight container.

HOW TO TAKE CHINESE TAKEOUT, LEFTOVER PIZZA, AND OTHER RIDICULOUS FOODS
INTO THE OUTDOORS

YOU MIGHT HAVE THE FALSE IMPRESSION THAT "HIKING" FOODS CAN ONLY BE BOUGHT in the same store where you buy backpacks and hiking boots. Although those stores do sell food items that are often tasty and contain extra calories, let me set you free of this misconception: You *can* take other foods, including perishable items, into the backcountry.

We usually have a couple hang-ups about taking food somewhere outside our house: (1) We think it can't survive very long without refrigeration before developing some sort of mold or turning into a hive of maggots, and (2) we're convinced that everything has to be consumed at the same temperature we would eat it in our home environment—i.e., a quesadilla should always be served hot off the griddle, and pasta salad should be chilled when eaten.

These are ideals, not requirements. Yes, if you take a block of Gouda and put it in a plastic bag in your backpack for ten days, it will likely spoil. But it can usually handle a day or three before becoming inedible. And after a few miles of hiking let me tell you, that quesadilla or pasta salad is going to taste good no matter the temperature.

Step outside of these two ideas you've lived by in the kitchen, and you can really begin to live in the outdoors. Let me tell you, the first time you bite into a slice of room-temperature pizza instead of a granola bar while you're enjoying a view from the top of the peak, the second half of your hiking life will begin. Keep in mind that on a day hike, your lunch only has to survive a few hours outside your refrigerator.

Some hiking food ideas:

Chinese takeout: If you go out to dinner a night or two before a hike, take half your dinner home with you. The morning of your hike, toss your leftovers in your backpack. Switch out the cardboard take-out box for a screw-top plastic container, which tends to be more watertight and won't leak sauce all over your backpack. Don't forget to take a fork or spoon (or chopsticks) with you in your pack, or you're going to be eating that sesame tofu with your fingers. Alternatively, if you're as good a cook as, say, the Chinese restaurant down the street from my house, cook your own meal and put some of the leftovers in the aforementioned screw-top plastic container.

Pizza: Put a couple slices of leftover delivery pizza in a gallon-size ziplock bag and take it in your pack. When it's not refrigerated, pizza tends to get mushy, so keep it at the top of your pack until it's time for lunch so that it doesn't get smashed into a ball while you're hiking. Another approach: One mountain guide I know bakes a full frozen pizza before four-day trips, cuts it into slices, puts it in a large ziplock bag, and keeps it in his backpack for lunch every day of that four-day trip. This works best in the cooler temperatures of spring and fall or at higher altitudes, where temperatures are lower.

Burritos: Grab a microwaveable burrito from the freezer aisle in your grocery store. The morning of your hike, throw it in an outside or top pocket of your backpack so the sun will thaw it as you hike (or warm it up on a hot day). Even fancier, take a travel-size bottle of hot sauce or packets of hot sauce from a fast-casual restaurant to add a little spice to your hiking lunch.

These are just a few ideas to get your brain thinking outside the box, or outside the energy bar aisle, as it were. Give them a try. If you can think of a food you enjoy in the city, you'll likely find a way to transport it while hiking. Ice cream is probably out, and biscuits and gravy might not travel that well, but keep an open mind and get creative. It's the outdoors, not outer space.

Pie: Fact #1: Humans have invented all shapes and sizes of sealable plastic containers. Fact #2: Some of these containers can fit a slice of cherry pie in them. Or apple pie, or whatever kind of pie you want. More than one company is currently making various flavors of "pie bar," and they're excellent. But let me tell you what's just as excellent: bringing a slice of pie in your backpack on a hike. Sure, it'll get jostled around a little bit, but not-exactly-perfectly-aesthetic pie on the summit of a mountain is still a wonderful thing, because guess what: It still tastes exactly like pie. Just don't forget an eating utensil.

Frosting: You may have noticed that several energy bar companies have worked to create easily transportable methods of sugar delivery for athletes—energy gels, chewy energy globules, and others. If you're not a weight-conscious ultrarunner or mountain biker, you can take a can of birthday cake frosting and a spoon with you. Spread it on some crackers and share with friends, or just eat it straight out of the can like the visionary you are. Be prepared to accept the stares of other curious—and jealous—hikers as they see what you're doing and their minds are blown.

—*Brendan*

CHOCOLATE CHIP COOKIE DOUGH
YOU COULD FRY BUT PROBABLY WON'T SINCE YOU'LL EAT IT ALL

Sucked in by the ideas of fresh cookies on a camping trip, we have fallen many times for a certain brand of prepackaged vegan, gluten-free cookie dough (as shown in this picture). Without eggs or butter, the cookie dough will keep, even if it isn't kept cold, for a few days.

But buying prepackaged gourmet cookie dough can get pricey, so we set out to make our own. We prefer to make ours with almond meal or finely ground almonds instead of flour, as it adds some nice texture to the dough. The result is so good we'd be surprised if it even made it as far as your frying pan; you'll be sneaking bites of this dough throughout the day as a snack.

MAKES Enough for 8–10 small cookies (if it lasts that long)

INGREDIENTS

1 cup almond meal or almond flour (You can make your own by finely grinding almonds in the food processor.)

¼ cup chocolate chips or chopped dark chocolate

¼ teaspoon salt

¼ teaspoon baking soda

2 tablespoons coconut oil

1 tablespoon maple syrup

¼ teaspoon vanilla extract

PREPARATION

AT HOME In a bowl, mix together the almond meal, chocolate, salt, and baking soda.

In a saucepan, melt the coconut oil. Remove from the heat and stir in the maple syrup and vanilla extract. Let cool for a few minutes. Pour the slightly cooled coconut oil into the almond meal mixture. Mix together and form into a log. If it's too sticky to form into a log, place in the refrigerator until it cools down a little and stiffens. Place the log into a plastic bag and chill in the refrigerator.

AT CAMP Eat the cookie dough on its own, or if you've managed to save some of it, place a frying pan on your stove. Slice the dough into rounds, and mold each round into a cookie shape. If the dough is cold and extra hard, it can get a little crumbly and just needs to be molded back together.

Fry the cookies in the frying pan for a couple of minutes on each side. Remove from the heat and let cool for a few minutes before serving.

CARROT CAKE BREAD
THAT IS NEITHER CAKE NOR BREAD

When you use a vegetable to make a baked good that's sweet and starchy, you can get away with calling it bread no matter how much sugar is in it. Why do you think people get so smug about eating zucchini bread? "Oh yeah, I LOVE zucchini." No you don't. You love having an excuse to eat cake disguised as a healthy food.

This recipe is neither cake nor bread. It's fluffy and moist and a little too sweet to be considered bread, but it's also healthier (hello nuts and yogurt!) and not so overly sweet as to really qualify as a cake. It's in that space in between: the space where you can feel good about eating more than one slice.

This not-quite-cake-not-quite-bread will serve you well as a breakfast treat on an early morning headed to the trailhead, or you can bring it on a chilly autumn hike paired with a large thermos of coffee or hot chocolate for a mid-trail snack.

INGREDIENTS

1½ cups whole-wheat flour
(For a gluten-free version, substitute 1 cup buckwheat flour and ½ cup rice flour.)

1 teaspoon baking powder

½ teaspoon baking soda

1 teaspoon cinnamon

1 teaspoon ground ginger

¼ teaspoon ground nutmeg

¼ teaspoon ground black pepper

1 egg

¼ cup olive oil

2–4 tablespoons honey
(depending on how sweet you want it)

½ cup plain yogurt

Zest of one small orange

2½ cups finely grated carrot

½ cup chopped walnuts

½ cup pepitas

½ cup raisins

PREPARATION

Preheat the oven to 375°F. Generously grease and flour a loaf pan.

In a large bowl, mix the dry ingredients.

In a separate bowl, whisk the egg; add the olive oil, honey, yogurt, and orange zest, and whisk until smooth. Add the wet mixture to the dry ingredients, along with the grated carrots, walnuts, pepitas, and raisins. Fold all the ingredients together.

Spoon the batter into the prepared bread loaf pan.

Bake for 40 to 50 minutes, until a knife inserted into the center of the loaf comes out clean. Remove from oven and let it cool before removing from the loaf pan.

SEASONAL FRUIT
HAND PIE

No matter what the season, pie is always in. But packing a pie in your backpack, kayak, pannier, or dog sled isn't always the simplest of affairs. That's why there's the hand pie: the modern adventurer's solution to transportable dessert (or breakfast if you're feeling cheeky).

The easiest way to create this recipe is to find yourself some seasonal fruit, buy a portion of pastry dough, and bake away. Of course if you want to go the 100 percent DIY route, we've included a recipe for a simple, slightly healthier pastry dough. Whole-wheat flour gives it a more robust taste, and the yogurt helps keep it nice and moist.

My favorite version of this recipe is with pears, but you can use whatever fruit you want—apples, blackberries, cherries, apricots. You can switch up the spice blend too, depending on what fruit you are using. If you don't have fresh fruit, jam will work well too.

MAKES 6–8 hand pies

INGREDIENTS

YOGURT PASTRY DOUGH

1 cup all-purpose flour

¾ cup whole-wheat flour

1 tablespoon sugar

¼ teaspoon salt

4 tablespoons butter, cold

¾ cup plain yogurt

SEASONAL FRUIT HAND PIE FILLING

1 portion pastry dough
(purchased or made using the ingredients above)

1–2 cups fruit
(Dice larger fruits, like pears and apples, into smaller pieces.)

1 teaspoon cinnamon

½ teaspoon cardamom

1 tablespoon sugar

PREPARATION

To make the dough, mix together the all-purpose flour, whole-wheat flour, sugar, and salt. Cut the butter into small cubes and work into the flour until the mixture is crumbly. Add the yogurt and mix together until you can form the dough into a ball. Knead and fold the dough a few times. Place in the refrigerator and let chill at least 30 minutes or overnight.

Preheat the oven to 375°F.

Place the diced fruit (no need to chop and dice if you are using berries) in a bowl along with the spices and sugar. Stir together so that the fruit is evenly covered.

Roll the pastry dough out to a large rectangle that is about 15 × 12 inches and a little less than ¼ inch thick. Cut the rectangle into 6 to 8 small rectangles.

Place some fruit mixture in the middle of each rectangle. If you have cut fairly narrow rectangles, it's easier to place the mixture on the bottom half of the rectangle. Leave a little room on the edges of the dough. Fill a bowl with cold water and dip your finger in it. Use your wet finger to brush the side of the dough with water. Then fold the dough over so that the edges align, and press the edges together.

Place pies on a baking tray lined with parchment paper or a silicone baking mat. Sprinkle the pies with cinnamon.

Bake for 30 to 40 minutes, until the hand pies are a deep golden brown. Remove from the oven and let cool before serving.

Store in an airtight container.

FRUIT BARS
THAT ARE NOT BAD FOR YOU BECAUSE, FRUIT

Fruit bars are basically an excuse to eat a double portion of dessert. But with these fruit bars, you can eat a triple portion, because they're low on sweetener and high on fruit. After all, do you really need an excuse to eat an extra treat while on the trail?

This recipe can be changed depending on what fruit is in season. Berries work well because you can easily mash them down, but if you're working with a harder fruit like apples, chop them as finely as you can, or consider cooking them down a little before adding them in. If you don't have fresh fruit on hand, Backpacker's Fruit Compote (page 174) makes an excellent replacement. Or you can use your favorite jam, as long as it has a thick consistency.

MAKES About 16 bars

INGREDIENTS

DOUGH

1½ cups whole-wheat flour

1 cup rolled oats

1 teaspoon salt

½ cup olive oil

3 tablespoons honey

½ teaspoon almond extract

1 egg, whisked

FILLING

About 1 cup fresh fruit

3 tablespoons ground flaxseeds or flax meal

2 tablespoons honey

PREPARATION

Preheat the oven to 400°F.

In a bowl, mix together the whole-wheat flour, oats, and salt. Add the olive oil, honey, and almond extract; mix together with a fork. Lightly whisk the egg and pour it over the mixture. Use your hands to work the dough together and form it into a ball.

Line a 9 × 9-inch pan with parchment paper. Press half the dough into the pan. The dough should reach all the way to the edges and be evenly pressed down.

To make the filling, mash the fruit; add the ground flaxseeds and honey. Mix together until well blended.

Evenly spread the fruit on the layer of dough. Take the other half of the dough, break it into small pieces, and scatter them over the top of the fruit. Lightly push the dough into the fruit.

Bake for 20 to 25 minutes, until golden brown.

Remove from the oven and let cool completely. Once cool, carefully lift the parchment paper and remove from the pan. Use a serrated knife to cut into bars.

HOW TO MAKE S'MORES
(BECAUSE EVERY CAMPING COOKBOOK EVER HAS TO INCLUDE A S'MORES RECIPE)

I DON'T WANT TO SOUND LIKE A CURMUDGEON HERE, but I would like to point out that you don't have to make s'mores when you go camping. I don't hate them (I hate the name), but I never make them. Just because something is a tradition doesn't mean you have to eat it—Christmas fruitcake, anyone?

There are far more interesting desserts you can make while camping, with or without a campfire. Recipes for some of those desserts are in this book. I think you should give them a shot before deciding to make s'mores for the hundredth time in your life.

But since this is an outdoor cookbook, if you really want to make s'mores, here's how to do it.

1. Start a campfire.

2. Get a stick, stab a marshmallow, and toast the marshmallow over the campfire.

3. Take a graham cracker, break it in half, and place a piece of chocolate on one half.

4. Place your toasted marshmallow on top of the piece of chocolate.

5. Take the other half of the graham cracker and place it on top of the marshmallow. Pull the stick out of the marshmallow. Now you have an adorable little graham cracker-chocolate-marshmallow sandwich.

6. Shove that little sugary sandwich in your face.

7. Remember to burn your marshmallow-smeared stick so the local wildlife doesn't get hold of it.

8. Put out your campfire.

—*Brendan*

DRIVE-THRU MOUNTAIN MORNING
BREAKFAST SANDWICHES

Whoever came up with the genius idea of eating sandwiches for breakfast deserves a medal—or, at the very least, a fan club. Breakfast sandwiches are just like regular sandwiches except they require an egg. Nothing beats the satisfaction of biting into a sandwich and having just a little yellow egg yolk run onto your hands. Tomatoes are a little fragile to take on a camping trip, but when they're in season, it's hard to resist. If you're looking for something other than tomatoes in your breakfast sandwich, you can try mushrooms, onions, red pepper, avocado, or anything your little breakfast-loving heart desires.

MAKES 1 sandwich

INGREDIENTS

1 egg

2 slices bread of your choice

Mustard

A few slices of hard cheese, like cheddar

1 small tomato, thinly sliced

Fresh basil leaves

MEAT OPTIONAL

PREPARATION

In a pan, fry the egg to your liking. (The runnier you leave it, the messier the eating process is going to be.)

Spread mustard on the two pieces of bread. Put one piece aside. On the other piece, layer a few slices of cheese, followed by half the tomato and the basil.

Add the egg and then layer the rest of the ingredients; top with the second piece of bread. You can put the sandwich into the frying pan for a bit to warm up the bread and slightly melt the cheese.

HOME ON THE FREE-RANGE
VEGGIE BURGERS

You like to feel wild and free in the outdoors, and so do your burgers. These veggie burgers require a can of black beans and one of our favorite tried-and-true camping staples: oats.

While black bean oatmeal might not be the breakfast of champions, these black bean oat burgers are an entirely different story; you'll probably forget you're even at the campsite. Serve them on their own and eat with a fork (you're camping, it's perfectly acceptable) or with a bun if you're packing that kind of thing. Hot sauce is definitely recommended.

MAKES 4–6 medium-size patties or 3 large ones

INGREDIENTS

1 (15-ounce) can black beans

1 teaspoon chipotle powder or cayenne pepper

1 teaspoon cumin powder

½ teaspoon salt

½ small onion, thinly sliced

½ cup quick cooking oats
(Use about ¼ cup more if using rolled oats.)

SUGGESTED TOPPINGS

Cheese

Avocado

Sautéed onions

Marinated mushrooms

Lettuce

Ample hot sauce

PREPARATION

Drain off the liquid from the can of beans and place them in a bowl. Mash together with a fork; add the spices and sliced onion and combine. Add the oats and stir until well blended. Let this mixture sit for about 10 minutes before cooking.

Place a frying pan over medium heat, and form the burger mixture into balls. If you don't want to get your hands dirty, you can use a spoon to place the batter in the frying pan and then form a patty with a spatula. Press down on the patties to flatten.

Fry the patties for 3 to 5 minutes on each side, until they are evenly baked. Top with your favorites.

SIMPLE MARINATED
MUSHROOMS

Mushrooms are a great addition to a lot of backcountry meals, not to mention they are delicious on their own. Try these on top of Clean Out the Cooler Vegetable Sauté (page XX), or just scramble some eggs and add these in for a killer breakfast. Even better, wrap all that goodness up in a tortilla and declare your mastery of the breakfast burrito game.

These are easy to prepare at home, throw in a sealable food container, and take with you; that will give them extra time to marinate. Sesame sauce might not be a regular ingredient in your spice kit, but consider adding it in; it adds a lot of flavor to many dishes, this one included. You can use whatever mushrooms you like, but this particular marinade works really well with shiitake mushrooms. If you're on a longer trip and can't bring fresh mushrooms, check out the instructions for cooking with dried mushrooms on page 181.

INGREDIENTS

About 2 cups sliced mushrooms

2 tablespoons soy sauce

3 tablespoons sesame oil

PREPARATION

Pack the sliced mushrooms into a sealable container. Drizzle the soy sauce and sesame oil on top. Seal the container and let marinate for at least 30 minutes before sautéing.

When ready to sauté the mushrooms, put a little olive oil or sesame oil in a pan and place on medium heat. Sauté the mushrooms for 3 to 5 minutes, until they have completely softened and decreased in size.

THERE ARE FEW THINGS
BETTER . . . THAN
BREAKFAST IN BED.

SPICY DAL
WITH KALE

Unlike other types of lentils, red lentils cook up fairly quickly, without needing to be soaked first. Dal, an Indian staple, is a great camping dish—it's hearty and will fill you up after a long day on the trail. This version gets a twist with the addition of kale. Of all vegetables, why kale? Eating fresh produce on trips can be difficult, as not all of it keeps well. Fortunately, unless you're trekking in extreme heat, a bag of kale leaves will survive a couple of days and can add some much-needed greenery to an outdoor meal. No greens on hand? Don't use that as an excuse to skip out on this dish; it's delicious with just the lentils too.

MAKES 2 servings

RATIO FOR COOKING LENTILS 1 part lentils to 3 parts water

INGREDIENTS

2 tablespoons olive oil

1–2 cloves garlic, finely chopped

1 teaspoon cumin powder

1 teaspoon coriander seeds (optional)

½ medium-size onion, finely chopped

½ serrano chile pepper, finely chopped (If you want the dish to be less spicy, remove the seeds before chopping.)

1 inch whole ginger, finely chopped

1½ cups water plus 2–3 tablespoons

½ cup red lentils

2–3 large kale leaves, finely chopped

Salt and pepper to taste

PREPARATION

In a pot, combine the olive oil and chopped garlic; place over medium heat. Let the garlic sizzle for about 1 minute before stirring in the cumin powder, coriander seeds, and chopped onion. Sauté for a minute or two. Add the chopped chile pepper and ginger; pour in 2 to 3 tablespoons of water and cover. Let simmer for 2 to 3 minutes. Add the lentils and remaining water. Stir together and cover.

Bring the contents of the pot to a boil and add the kale leaves. Cook 10 to 15 minutes, until the lentils are tender and have soaked up almost all the water (the consistency should be thick). Stir every once in a while to make sure the lentils are not sticking to the bottom of the pan. If you want them a bit thicker and mushier, cook a little longer.

THE JOY OF
SLOWING DOWN

MAN, COOKING IN THE OUTDOORS IS A REAL PAIN, ISN'T IT? You have to go get water from a lake or stream. There's no sink to do dishes in. You don't have all the utensils you'd have at home, nor do you have space to prep everything. And when you're done eating, you have to put everything away so bears don't get it (or get you). I mean, what's the point?

Have you ever wondered if every year of your life seems to be getting shorter and shorter? That you have less time to get everything done. That you never have time to do the things you'd like to do. That there's always an e-mail you need to respond to, no matter how many e-mails you've already responded to that day? Yeah, me too.

It is no coincidence that we've convinced ourselves we don't have any time to cook real food anymore. We need prepackaged meals that we can pop in the microwave, drive-thru restaurants, even pre-chopped vegetables or preassembled meal plans that are shipped to us—right down to the wine that complements the entree.

We need to slow down every once in a while and go someplace where it's a complete pain to do even the slightest of food preparation tasks. To live off very few items, carry only what you need, and try not to do five things at once for a day or two.

When you're in the backcountry, you need to not only accept that dinner (and breakfast) are going to take an inconveniently long time, but revel in it. Sit on a rock or a log. Don't do anything but cook. Watch the clouds move and the sky turn colors as the sun rises or sets; listen to the wind in the trees or the water rushing through the creek. Remind yourself that any hour you can spend like this is better than an hour of reading e-mails, sitting in meetings, or watching TV.

Dinner will take a while to cook, and that's fine, because you probably have two things on your schedule for the rest of the day: Eat dinner and then crawl into your sleeping bag for the night. If you're feeling ambitious, maybe schedule "tea" or a "nip of whiskey" after dinner— but don't get too carried away.

Feel that? That's the feeling of having nothing to do, of all your stress hormone levels tapering off. You're in the middle of nowhere, (hopefully) without a cell phone signal, eating dinner. And since no one can contact you, you've pulled yourself out of the faster-faster-faster stream of society, if only for just a couple days.

The more you camp, the more (I hope) you'll learn to make dinner last as long as possible: gathering water, maybe making soup, then the main course, a little dessert, and then some tea or spirits after dinner while the sun sets and you start feeling yourself getting drowsy.

The go-go-go speed of our "real world" is great for a lot of things—just not the cooking and eating experience. Let's learn to enjoy dinner in the backcountry and then take that feeling back home with us when we leave. Because you're going to be back in your universe of faster-faster-faster soon enough, and you'll probably realize that it is way too soon.

—*Brendan*

MULTI-DAY
OUTINGS

THREE-INGREDIENT (BESIDES PEANUTS)
PEANUT SAUCE

Whether you're making the camp version of pad thai or just need something to douse your bottom-of-the-cooler vegetables in, peanut sauce is a versatile sauce that you might just eat with a spoon.

To simplify your peanut butter sauce–making experience, prep the soy sauce and sesame oil at home. Pour them into a small bottle, and all you have to do when it comes time to make your sauce is dump them in the pan.

We've designed this recipe with as few ingredients as possible, but if you want to add a little extra flavor, toss in a teaspoon of ground ginger (or a tablespoon of freshly chopped ginger) and two teaspoons of chili powder.

MAKES About 2 servings

INGREDIENTS

4 teaspoons soy sauce

2 teaspoons sesame oil

¼ cup peanut butter

2–4 tablespoons water

PREPARATION

Place the soy sauce, sesame oil, and peanut butter in a pan on low to medium heat. Stir until the peanut butter softens. If you like a really thick sauce, stop here. If you want it a little runnier, add the water, pouring slowly until the sauce reaches the desired consistency.

EASY PINE NUT AND PESTO
PASTA

Seriously, your idiot roommate from college who couldn't manage to replace the toilet paper in the bathroom, get to class on time, or make proper macaroni and cheese from a box could handle this recipe. It may sound fancy, but it's not hard to make. Have we established that point enough? It will also impress the folks you're backpacking with, because it's a nice, savory pasta dish with the super-protein and minerals of a big fistful of pine nuts (and you don't have to cart in a jar of sauce to make it). This recipe is high in calories, perfect for a dinner after a long day of hiking, and before the next long day of hiking.

OK, enjoy it. You got this.

MAKES 2 servings

INGREDIENTS

8 ounces fusilli pasta

1 ounce olive oil

1 (0.5-ounce) package powdered basil pesto pasta mix

1 cup pine nuts

PREPARATION

Estimate enough water to cover pasta (probably 32 ounces or so) and bring it to a boil.

Add pasta, return to boil, cover pot, and reduce heat to low. Cook pasta for 5 minutes; turn off the heat and let it soak for another 5 minutes, or until pasta is al dente.

Stir in olive oil and pesto mix. After pesto is evenly blended into pasta, stir in pine nuts. Enjoy.

MEAT OPTIONAL

DIY SPICY
HOT CHOCOLATE MIX

The world was drinking hot chocolate long before people took it on camping trips as an evening pick-me-up. In fact, people have been drinking chocolate for thousands of years. It was popular in Mesoamerica, and the Aztecs commonly added chile pepper to the drink. And while they preferred their drink cold, that spicy hot chocolate flavor is one that stuck and is still popular today.

This drink is in homage to those earlier versions—not as sweet, and thicker because of the addition of real chocolate and not just cocoa powder like you find in most mixes. The cinnamon brings in an extra element of spice, but you can leave it out if you want to stick to chili powder. Want the hot chocolate a little smoky? Chipotle chili powder is good too.

MAKES 6–8 cups hot chocolate

INGREDIENTS

1 cup finely chopped dark chocolate

¼ cup cane sugar

½ cup unsweetened cocoa powder

1 teaspoon chili powder

1 teaspoon ground cinnamon (optional)

PREPARATION

In a bowl, mix all the ingredients together.

Double or triple the batch, depending on the length of your trip or how many people are going to be drinking your hot chocolate. Place your mix in a sealable bag or container.

To make the hot chocolate, use 3 to 4 tablespoons for 1 cup of boiling water. If you want your hot chocolate to be sweeter, you can add a little more sugar to the mix or stir in some honey when you brew it.

THE IMPORTANCE OF
HOT BEVERAGES

CONTRARY TO POPULAR BELIEF, HOT DRINKS DON'T ACTUALLY WARM YOU THAT MUCH. If you're already warm, studies show that hot beverages will actually cool your body temperature down a little bit.

So why should you waste your time making hot drinks? Climbers on big mountain routes will often stop to "brew up" or make a quick cup of hot tea. And you'd have a hard time convincing me not to drink a cup of ginger tea before I hop in my sleeping bag for a cold night under the stars.

I can't argue against scientific studies, but I will argue for the placebo effect. If I think I'm getting warm drinking hot tea outside my tent as the temperature rapidly drops, I feel warmer. Science also says that your ability to deal with cold temperatures is mostly in your head. Obviously, the right clothing plays a part (as well as staying dry), but if you want to increase your tolerance to cold temperatures, the tried-and-true method is to spend more time in cold temperatures. And spend that time telling yourself, "This isn't that bad."

So hot tea, hot chocolate, and hot coffee are all weapons in my personal quest to have more fun in the cold.

You might think a little nip of whiskey is good for those cold evenings on your backpacking and camping trips, right? Wrong. There are plenty of reasons to drink liquor, but increasing your body temperature isn't one of them. Alcohol actually lowers your body's temperature and dehydrates you, two things that don't help you during chilly nights sleeping under the stars. Liquor isn't dangerous per se, but maybe not worth the weight.

Tea bags, however, are lightweight, and a cup of non-caffeinated tea will help hydrate you before a long night in a sleeping bag, during which you will lose water just by breathing cool air.

My favorite cold-night after-dinner tea is any sort of lemon ginger—ginger, unlike alcohol and hot drinks, has been proven to increase body temperature. And I was not a tea drinker until way later in life, when I realized how great it was to hold a steaming mug of hot liquid during the last few minutes of an evening in the mountains or desert and sip it while trying to get psyched to zip myself into my tent and sleeping bag for the night

And I'll tell you what: It's always worked, because I always tell myself it works. That's the placebo effect: Does it increase body temperature and therefore warmth? That's inconclusive at best. Does it increase morale, and therefore my ability to psychologically handle cold temperatures? Yes it does, because I said so.

—Brendan

NUT AND SEED
PARM

Sure, you could buy that green cardboard cylinder of "Parmesan" cheese to stuff in your food bag, but despite what the "100 percent cheese" marketing says, who knows what you're going to be eating?

Better to make your own salty topping that's not only tasty but also vegan-friendly. Consider this nut and seed parm your new best friend in the outdoor kitchen. It makes pretty much anything better (we have yet to put it in hot chocolate, but who knows). Nutty and salty, it has that umami flavor that we often crave when we're tired after a day of adventuring. A bowl of pasta? Douse it in nut and seed parm. Couscous? Douse it in nut and seed parm. Bored with your morning oatmeal and want to turn it into a savory breakfast? Douse it in nut and seed parm. Nothing else to eat? Grab a spoon and eat your nut and seed parm on its own.

You can use any combination of nuts and seeds for this recipe, but hazelnuts work particularly well. If you want to skip the seeds and go 100 percent nuts, by all means, have at it.

MAKES ¾ cup

INGREDIENTS

¼ cup nuts, like hazelnuts or almonds

¼ cup seeds, like sunflower or pumpkin seeds

¼–½ teaspoon sea salt
(depending on how salty you want it)

PREPARATION

Preheat oven to 375°F.

In a baking pan, toast the nuts and seeds for 5 to 10 minutes. The nuts and seeds should get slightly darker in color, but be careful not to let them burn. Remove from the oven and let cool for a few minutes.

Place the nuts, seeds, and salt in a food processor and mix together until finely ground.

Store in an airtight container.

CHEESY
COUSCOUS

Do you love macaroni and cheese but wish it were more nutritious? Are you slightly self-conscious about cooking a dish that you loved when you were eight years old? Do you feel like an adult's dinner should be a little less orange?

Hey. Don't be self-conscious. Macaroni and cheese is pretty awesome, whether you're eight or eighty. But it could be a tad bit more nutritious with vegetables, maybe a little protein. If only there was a way to create this cheesy dish in the backcountry without wasting a ton of backpacking stove gas trying to get your pasta to be al dente.

Allow me to introduce you to cheesy couscous, long endorsed by top alpinists and discerning backpackers alike. It won't take up much space in your pack, it's full of nutrients (and calories!), and it's easy to make, whether you're sitting on a rock next to your tent by an alpine lake or hanging off the side of El Capitan in a portaledge.

MAKES 2 servings

INGREDIENTS

6 ounces sharp cheddar cheese

2 cups water

2 tablespoons olive oil

½ cup dehydrated soup vegetables

1½ cups couscous

MEAT OPTIONAL

PREPARATION

Slice the cheese into small cubes (thin wafers, rectangles, polygons, octagons, or whatever shape you think will melt the quickest when it's time to add it).

Pour the water, olive oil, and soup vegetables into the pot and bring the water to a boil. You're rehydrating the soup vegetables so that they won't crunch. When the water reaches a full boil, stir in the couscous. Cover the pot, turn off the stove, and wait 5 minutes. Use this time to talk to your hiking partner about the book you're reading or your favorite podcast episode of all time. If you're by yourself, stare off into space and think about how far away you are from your closest friend and what he or she might be doing at that moment.

After 5 minutes, the couscous should have absorbed all the water. Stir in your cheese shapes until the cheese is melted and distributed throughout. Serve and enjoy.

NO SHIT, YOU CAN MAKE YOUR OWN
TRAIL MIX

Here's what happens whenever you buy a bag of trail mix at the store: It's good enough, and you like most of the ingredients, but there's always one thing in there that you don't like, and you have to either choke it down or throw away what's left of it when you get to the bottom of the bag. Every time you pull that bag of trail mix out of your backpack, you wonder, "Why did they include [Ingredient X]? I hate those things." And there they are, ruining your snacks.

Well, it's about time you took responsibility for your own happiness, and here's your chance. That's right, you're going to make your own trail mix, because (a) it's not that hard, (b) life's too short to eat food you don't like when you're hiking, and (c) you're an adult. All you need is access to a grocery store that sells nuts, fruits, and candy in bulk. If you can find one of those, you've pushed through the crux of this mission.

MAKES Enough for a day or a week, depending on how much of each ingredient you buy

INGREDIENTS

1 part your favorite nut (for protein and fat); example: cashews

1 part your second favorite nut or favorite seed (for protein and fat); example: pumpkin seeds

1 part your favorite dried fruit (to make this seem at least a little healthy); example: dried cherries

1 part your favorite bite-size chocolate; example: dark chocolate chips

1 part your favorite bite-size candy; example: M&Ms or Reese's Pieces

PREPARATION

Get a ziplock bag big enough to hold all the combined ingredients you've purchased for your trail mix. Pour in all five ingredients, close the ziplock opening, and knead the contents with your fingers until they're evenly mixed. Open the bag, grab a fistful of trail mix, and pour it into your mouth. Chew and reflect on what a culinary genius you are for coming up with this wonderful trail mix recipe.

"LIFE'S TOO SHORT
TO EAT FOOD YOU
DON'T LIKE."

TRAIL MIX
PANCAKES

No matter how delicious your trail mix, by Day Four or Five you are totally over it. Thankfully, a handful of trail mix can make for a more interesting breakfast. Combine it with some oats and pancake mix and you've got a hearty batch of pancakes. Not only will they serve as breakfast, but if you make a few extra and stash them in a bag (or a pocket), they will come in handy as a trail snack later in the day.

INGREDIENTS

1 cup DIY pancake mix (page 90)

¼ cup oats

Large handful of trail mix

About 1 cup water

Oil for frying pan (if necessary)

PREPARATION

Mix together the dry pancake mix with the oats and trail mix. Add in the water, a little at a time. Go slowly so that you can get the right consistency; it's easier to add a little more water than it is to add more dry mix. If you're using quick-cooking oats, they will soak up water very quickly and you may need to add a little more water to get the right consistency. Mix together until smooth.

Place a frying pan over medium heat; add a little oil if needed. Place a spoonful of batter into the frying pan. Once the pancake is firm around the edges and bubbles pop in the middle, flip it over and cook until done. Serve immediately. Or let cool and store in your pocket for pocket pancakes somewhere down the trail.

BREAKFAST IN BED
MAKES YOU A BETTER LOVER

YOU'VE HAD A TYPICAL NIGHT OF TENT SLEEPING: It took you hours to fall asleep, and when you finally did, it was a fitful sleep, your mind more aware of the moments when you awkwardly tried to turn in your sleeping bag than of dreamtime. As night turned to dawn, your body finally decided it could sleep—and suddenly it's morning.

Now you smell coffee.

You slowly open those sleepy eyes. The tent is bright, fully lit with daylight. You look next to you. There is no sign of your partner except for a ruffled sleeping bag, pushed halfway down the sleeping pad. You hear the tent door unzip. A hand sticks in. It's holding a coffee mug.

"Breakfast is on the way. Here's coffee to tide you over."

There are few things better on trips than someone making you breakfast in bed. Or "in tent," as the case may be. The love and care that go into pulling oneself out of a warm sleeping bag to prepare breakfast in the cold, solo, is a heartfelt act that never goes unnoticed. And if it does, you should seriously consider finding another partner.

Serving breakfast in bed makes you a better lover. Breakfast in bed is the outdoor world's version of sexy lingerie. Except unlike sexy lingerie, breakfast is practical, never verges on looking ridiculous, and doesn't come with special washing instructions. Hold a plate of breakfast in your hand and unzip that tent door, and you have never looked better.

Of course making someone breakfast in bed in the outdoors involves some stealth. If you want it to be a surprise, you'll have to ensure that your partner is fast asleep, or at least has earplugs so he or she won't hear you crawl out of the tent. It's best if you thought about setting out the breakfast foods and utensils the night before so that you don't have to go clambering through all your gear to find them. The sound of water boiling for coffee might wake your partner up, but by that point, you've already started the process. Sipping on a cup of coffee in his or her sleeping bag while waiting for you to concoct breakfast is a glorious moment your partner will not soon forget.

When you cook someone breakfast in bed in the outdoors, no matter where you are, you're sure to have a day full of exciting adventures.

Today will be exciting. Today the breakfast will be served. And today you will be known as the best lover on the planet. All because you crawled out of your sleeping bag a little early. Seems like a small sacrifice to make, doesn't it?

—Anna

MOUNTAIN CLIMBER'S
OATMEAL

This is called Mountain Climbers' Oatmeal because in general, instant oatmeal is gross. Store-bought instant oatmeal seems like a good idea for breakfast while you're backpacking; the serving size is measured out for you, and it seems easy to pack one packet of oatmeal for each morning, right? Wrong. There are about 160 to 200 calories in a single packet of typical instant oatmeal, which is about enough fuel to walk from your car to the office and sit on your ass answering e-mails until lunch. That's not nearly enough calories to do anything significant in the outdoors, other than start walking on a trail and then stop after a half-mile to dig out your trail mix because you're starving.

This recipe adds some calories, fat, and protein to oatmeal so that you can get a little farther up the trail before you start thinking about lunch. You don't have to be climbing a mountain to eat it.

MAKES Enough for 1 person

RATIO FOR COOKING OATMEAL 1 part oats to 2 parts water

INGREDIENTS

½ cup water

2 tablespoons powdered peanut butter

¼ cup oatmeal

¼ cup walnuts

¼ cup pumpkin seeds

¼ cup dried cherries

PREPARATION

Boil water.

Mix powdered peanut butter and oatmeal together in a bowl.

Pour boiling water over peanut butter and oatmeal mixture; stir together.

Stir in walnuts, pumpkin seeds, and dried cherries.

Eat, go crush that trail, and enjoy not collapsing from hunger before midmorning.

MOUNTAIN CLIMBER'S OATMEAL
FOR MOUNTAIN CLIMBERS WITH A SWEET TOOTH

If you have a sweet tooth, this oatmeal will make you happier than a nine-year-old sitting in front of the TV watching *Super Friends* with a box of Cocoa Puffs, a carton of milk, and no supervision. I'm not saying it will stick with you all morning, but if you're planning on burning calories first thing after breakfast, what's wrong with pounding some candy in the morning? You're going to put on your pack and walk off some of those calories.

MAKES Enough for 1 person

RATIO FOR COOKING OATMEAL 1 part oats to 2 parts water

INGREDIENTS

½ cup water

2 tablespoons powdered peanut butter

¼ cup oatmeal

¼ chocolate bar

¼ cup M&M's or other candy

¼ cup walnuts

PREPARATION

Boil water.

Mix powdered peanut butter and oatmeal together in a bowl.

Pour boiling water over peanut butter and oatmeal mixture; stir together.

Break chocolate bar into pieces and stir into oatmeal. Garnish with M&M's and walnuts.

Eat, go crush that trail, and enjoy not collapsing from hunger before midmorning.

MOUNTAIN CLIMBER'S OATMEAL
FOR MOUNTAIN CLIMBERS WHO PREFER SAVORY

If you've packed a large bag of oats for a trip, one thing is certain: There will come a day when you will rise from your slumber and murmur, "I cannot eat another bowl of oatmeal." You can, and you will, but it doesn't have to be the standard version. Since you've been spending the last few days seeing how much cinnamon is too much, why not skip the sweet version of oatmeal entirely? A few lightweight savory ingredients and you've got a bowl of oatmeal that's a little out of the ordinary. And on Day Six, that's exactly what you need.

MAKES 1 serving

RATIO FOR COOKING OATMEAL 1 part oats to 2 parts water

INGREDIENTS

½ cup water

¼ cup oatmeal

3–4 sundried tomatoes

Handful of pumpkin seeds

2 teaspoons dried garlic flakes

Salt

Pepper

PREPARATION

Prepare oats as you would for Mountain Climber's Oatmeal.

Add savory ingredients and stir. If you want your sundried tomatoes rehydrated, add them to your dry oats before you add the water.

NO ONE CARES
ABOUT YOUR DUTCH OVEN PHOTOS

HEY, OUTDOOR FOOD LOVER. YEAH, I'M TALKING TO YOU.

I see you there with your gorgeous "wild" food photos. Cradling your coffee mug while you're smugly (yeah, I said "smug" and not "snug") wrapped in your Pendleton blanket. That amazing collaborative meal you cooked in your Dutch oven.

No one cares about your Dutch oven photos.

Sure, they look tasty, and I bet your blackberry cobbler with freshly foraged fruit and hand-ground oat flour was delicious. But let's get real. You did not hike into the backcountry with that thing.

I like cast iron as much as the next person, but when I see "50 Great Meals to Make Outdoors" articles and forty-nine of them are made in a Dutch oven, I wonder who tested the recipes. If you're cooking with a full-scale kitchen, you're not cooking outside.

Hey, I get it. Dutch ovens are great. I can support those of you who take them on trips where weight isn't an issue. Chili made in a Dutch oven overlooking the river? I am all for it.

But the rest of you "glampers" can stay home.

Using a Dutch oven does not mean you #liveauthentic. You might as well have walked out your backdoor and started a campfire. And if you did, good on you. I'd never turn down a chance to eat food outside, even if I was steps away from my front door. Bare feet in the grass and a bowl of something tasty in your hands is an amazing experience, no matter where.

But I see you there, trying to make other people think you made it out to some incredible, wild place; saw things no one has ever seen before; wrote in your journal while listening to the creek and watching the sunrise; ate your steaming bowl of oatmeal while you sat perfectly clothed with your floppy brimmed hat in the doorway of your tent; had your soul touched by the beauty and stillness that can only be felt in the wilderness. And you brought your Dutch oven? I doubt it.

You hiked in with that thing strapped to your backpack? Apparently weight is no concern when you know the healing benefits of a quality meal outside. I bet you even brought twine to wrap around your sandwiches and sprigs of rosemary to make your s'mores look tastier.

I want none of it. Absolutely none of it.

Except for maybe that wool blanket.

And that coffee mug.

And your Dutch oven blackberry cobbler. With some hand-whipped cream please. You brought that along too, didn't you?

—Anna

WHEN IT'S APPROPRIATE TO START TALKING ABOUT
REAL FOOD ON THE TRAIL

WE'VE COME A LONG WAY AS A SPECIES WHEN IT COMES TO EATING AND LIVING OUTSIDE.
We've gone from caves to ultralight $350 tents, from hardened calluses on our feet to high-tech hiking boots, and from hunting with spears and gathering berries and edible plants to making fancy pasta meals with a tiny stove and some hot water.

But that doesn't mean that when you're on the trail and letting your mind wander, your mind isn't going to wander to visuals of french fries, nachos, ice cream, and cold beer. It is. It's only a matter of time, really—the same way your brain is going to start delivering images of your pillow-top mattress and high-thread-count duvet or a warm shower with high water pressure. You probably will fantasize about "real food" before the bed and the shower.

This is perfectly natural, and nothing to be ashamed of. Should you do anything about it? I recommend trying to keep it under control. My personal rule on any adventure, whether it's a day or a month long, is the Halfway Rule: Don't start talking about anything back in the "real world" until you're at least halfway through whatever it is you're doing. If you're on a 6-mile hike, wait to mention burritos until mile 3. If you're on a weeklong backpacking trip, wait until after lunch on Day Four to talk about the cheeseburger and beer you're going to have as soon as you get your boots off your feet and drive to the nearest town.

This rule keeps me optimistic through the first half of anything by keeping me in the moment; and in the second half, it motivates me with the anticipation of a reward at the end. If your brain works a little differently, you'll want to come up with your own rule. Maybe you want to wait until the evening before your last day on the trail to bring up the post-adventure binge meal. Or wait until the trailhead parking lot to say, "So, guys, how about we get a pizza on our way home?" But I strongly suggest you wait until at least halfway. Nobody wants to be on a trip with someone who's already talking about "going home" the minute he or she steps on the trail—that low-grade pessimism says "I really don't want to be here" or "I'm not excited about this and my mind is already fantasizing about being done."

So don't be that guy or girl. Find some joy in the food you've brought (purchasing this cookbook should help), bring some small things that are mental rewards, and at whatever point you've decided it's OK, give yourself that mental carrot to get you to the finish line, whether it's nachos, pizza, burritos, beer, or a hot shower. Or imagine all five of those things simultaneously, if you have a really roomy shower that will allow you to keep the nachos somewhat dry.

—Brendan

BACKPACKER'S
FRUIT COMPOTE

Fresh fruit might not be an option on longer backcountry trips, but chances are you've got a bit of dried fruit stashed somewhere in your backpack. However, as any outdoor adventurer knows, the dried fruit routine can get a little old after a few days. This recipe helps you deal with that problem, bringing some life back into your fruit. The compote can be eaten on its own, served over pancakes, mixed into oatmeal, or served with a few pieces of dark chocolate for the ultimate backcountry dessert. You can use any dried fruit you have with you. Our two favorite combinations are apricot and fig and cherries and blueberries. Close your eyes and you might just think you're at the fruit stand.

MAKES 2–3 servings

INGREDIENTS

1 cup dried fruit (If you are using large pieces of dried fruit, like apricots and figs, cut them into smaller pieces; this will make for a smoother compote.)

About 1 cup water

PREPARATION

Place the dried fruit in a water bottle or cup. Cover with water until fruit is fully submerged. Let soak for at least 30 minutes. Pro tip: Place the fruit and water in a water bottle before you go to bed, close it up, and come morning you'll be ready to cook the compote right away.

Pour the fruit and water into a pot and place over medium heat. Let the fruit simmer, regularly stirring and mashing down any large pieces of fruit. Allow a few minutes to cook down. The compote is done when the consistency is to your liking.

SUPER FANCY TOASTED
WALNUT COUSCOUS

Put nuts into a bowl full of grains and you have a dish of grains and nuts. Toast your nuts beforehand and you've just elevated that meal to super tasty status. Partnered with one of the easiest grains to cook—if you can boil water, you can make couscous—this is a quick meal that you don't have to spend too much time thinking about. The dried red pepper (which is lightweight and backpacking recipe friendly) adds some additional color and taste. There's no reason backcountry cooking should be bland. If you don't have walnuts, just reach into your trail mix bag and grab whatever nuts are on hand.

MAKES 2 servings

RATIO FOR COOKING COUSCOUS 3 parts couscous to 4 parts water

INGREDIENTS

½ cup walnuts

1 cup water

2 tablespoons dried red pepper

¾ cup couscous

2 teaspoons dried minced garlic

¼ teaspoon salt

1–2 tablespoons olive oil

MEAT OPTIONAL

PREPARATION

Place the walnuts in a pot over your stove. Toast them, shaking the pot regularly to move them around, until they start to turn a dark brown. They will burn quickly, so keep an eye on them.

Once the walnuts are toasted, transfer them to a bowl. Add the water and red pepper to your pot, and bring to a boil. Remove from the heat and pour in the couscous, minced garlic, and salt. Stir together and cover. Let sit for about 10 minutes, until the couscous has softened.

Add the toasted walnuts and olive oil, and stir together. Spoon into bowls and serve.

CLOSE-ENOUGH-TO-PAD-THAI
PAD THAI

Pad thai is one of those dishes that most of us are far more apt to get for takeaway than we are to make at home. It's a simple dish of stir-fried noodles, but if you make it for your friends, you're immediately the master of the kitchen. Imagine what would happen if you made it on a camp stove. Let's get one thing clear: This isn't traditional pad thai. There's no fish sauce and no fried egg. But what do people love about pad thai? The stir-fried rice noodles with peanuts scattered on top, which is exactly what this dish is. Close enough? That's a recipe that's just right.

This recipe uses another one of our standards: Three-Ingredient (besides Peanuts) Peanut Sauce (page 144). On shorter trips—one or two nights—you can get away with packing tofu, and it's worth it. The same goes for the green onion and cilantro. To make cooking easy, you can pre-chop the green onions and store them in a small bag until it's time to cook. Out on a longer adventure? Just toss in more peanuts. You could also pack dried cilantro and dried green onions, store-bought or homemade.

MAKES 2 servings

INGREDIENTS

1 serving Three-Ingredient (besides Peanuts) Peanut Sauce

1–2 cups water

6 ounces rice noodles

2–3 tablespoons olive oil

2 gloves garlic, finely chopped

2 teaspoons hot sauce or chili powder

About 7 ounces firm tofu, cut into small cubes (optional)

¼ cup peanuts, chopped

1 green onion, finely chopped (optional)

Handful of fresh cilantro leaves (optional)

PREPARATION

Make the peanut sauce and set aside while you prep the noodles.

Boil the water; remove the pot from the stove, and place the noodles in the hot water. Cover and let stand for about 5 minutes.

While the noodles are soaking, in another pot or frying pan, add the olive oil and garlic and sauté until the garlic turns golden. Add the hot sauce and tofu, and fry for another 1 to 2 minutes.

Drain the noodles (save the water for an after-dinner hot chocolate) and add to the mixture in the other pan. Stir regularly for about 1 minute. Add the peanut sauce and tofu; stir together until the noodles are coated.

Remove from the stove. Serve in bowls and top with peanuts, green onion, and cilantro leaves.

NO PUFFY JACKET REQUIRED
DRIED MUSHROOM PASTA

This isn't as much a recipe as a guide. We assume that you know how to make pasta, because if you don't, it's shocking that you have made it this far.

But do you know how to cook with dried mushrooms? Dried mushrooms are one of the easiest and lightest ways to add flavor to pasta when camping. In a normal kitchen (one you didn't pack on your back), it's suggested that you give dried mushrooms ample time to soak so that they can fully rehydrate and keep their flavor. Well we're not in a traditional kitchen now, are we? To save on time—*and* ensure that your mushrooms rehydrate enough that your system will still be happy once you're finished eating—you want to do two things:

> Break your mushrooms into smaller pieces; they will rehydrate better.
> Add the mushrooms to the water *before* you put it on the stove. This allows the rehydrating mushrooms to spend a lot of time in the water as it comes to a boil and afterward as you boil your pasta.

What kind of mushrooms should you buy? The main thing to keep in mind when purchasing, other than taste, is that the thicker the dried mushrooms, the longer they will take to rehydrate. Morels, porcinis, and chanterelles work well for this particular recipe, and all three rehydrate in the time it takes to boil the pasta.

Another benefit of boiling your water with the mushrooms in it from the beginning? You'll end up with starchy, mushroomy pasta water at the end of it. Don't you dare throw that away! On a cold evening, this makeshift mushroom broth is a delicious treat.

Besides mushrooms, the sky is the limit for whatever you want to add to your pasta. A sprinkling of cheese or Nut and Seed Parm (page 152) after your pasta is ready to serve will add some additional umami flavor. Spice it up with red pepper flakes or, if you want a tamer, more traditional pasta flavor, dried basil leaves.

MAKES 2 servings

INGREDIENTS

2 servings dry pasta of your choice

½ ounce dried mushrooms of your choice

Olive oil

OPTIONAL

Small chunk of hard cheese or Nut and Seed Parm

Finely chopped garlic

Red pepper flakes

Dried basil leaves

PREPARATION

Measure out the appropriate amount of water for your pasta and place in a pot with the mushrooms. Place on the stove and bring to a boil. Let the water boil for a couple of minutes before adding the pasta (this will give the mushrooms a little extra time to rehydrate). Add the pasta and cook until tender.

When the pasta has finished cooking, pour off the water into a water bottle or camp cups to save.

Drizzle a little olive oil over the pasta and whatever other ingredients you want to add. Stir together to fully coat the pasta. Spoon into bowls and serve.

YOU TOO CAN KICK
THE FREEZE-DRIED HABIT

GROWING UP, THERE WAS ALWAYS A BAG OF FREEZE-DRIED FOODS with our camp supplies—a selection of packaged, instant meals that were intended for "just in case" situations. We rarely dove into them, and they became part of the food-packing list more out of habit than out of desire. Then one summer I decided we should try the beef Stroganoff, just to see what it tasted like.

Never. Again.

While the quality of freeze-dried and dehydrated foods has improved exponentially in the past decade, there is still no excuse for not making your own food. Weight? Few of you are taking the kinds of trips that necessitate cutting off the ends of toothbrushes. Even when you are, there are perfectly easy-to-make, lightweight meals that won't cost you an arm and a leg and won't lead to a ridiculous amount of waste. Remember that you have to pack out all of those empty food pouches.

Let's be honest with ourselves: The freeze-dried food habit has very little to do with what food weighs. No, it's all about laziness. In a fast-food culture, we have grown accustomed to ordering something, waiting a few minutes, and then diving in. And why should the wilderness be any different? This is America, and if you can't hike and eat an instant meal, then what's the point?

The point is that we're missing the point. Boil water, pour into pouch, seal, wait 20 minutes. What are you going to do with those extra 20 minutes? Sit by the river and meditate? Highly unlikely. Write compelling Instagram captions that you can post when you get home? Probably. Connect to your satellite phone so that you can actually update your social media with one of those captions? Most definitely.

Why not spend those 20 minutes cooking? Why not get your adventuring partner in crime to help you? Cooking is an enriching social activity, even at the end of those long days when you really don't want to be bothered. And if you're not interested in the social benefits of meals, focus on taste instead.

We have such a craving for instant food that we don't even care about quality. "Yeah, this is OK," we say as we try the latest instant meal, knowing perfectly well that the bar is set ridiculously low. If we were served something similar at home, we wouldn't even touch it. Why not make meals that get you to say, "This is delicious!"

Shouldn't you have an outdoor life that's a little more full of "hell yeah's" instead of "ok's"?

You too can kick the freeze-dried habit, but it will require accepting that some of your habits from everyday modern life have crept into your outdoor life as well. Challenge yourself to not seek out instant gratification. Remember that an outdoor meal doesn't have to be extravagant to taste excellent.

—Anna

THERE ARE NO LEFTOVER TORTILLAS
NACHOS

If you've ever brought tortillas as a lunch component on a trip, you know what happens a few days in: You've enjoyed a few tortillas spread thick with peanut butter and honey, and now you're stuck with a bag of broken, dried-out tortilla bits that no one wants to eat. Yet.

There's one easy way to bring a tortilla back to life: Fry it. Have a hunk of hard cheese floating around the bottom of your food bag? Even better—you can make nachos.

These makeshift nachos are everything you want nachos to be: oily, crispy, and cheesy. If you've got salsa on hand, add some of that on top too.

INGREDIENTS

Tortillas, cut into strips

Olive oil for frying

Cumin powder (optional)

Red pepper flakes (optional)

Cheese, cut into small pieces

PREPARATION

If you have somehow managed to keep your tortillas in regular form, cut them into small strips. Pour some olive oil into a pan or pot so that the bottom is evenly covered. Add some cumin powder and red pepper flakes if you like. Place on medium heat.

Once the oil is warm, add your tortilla strips. Stir regularly so that the tortilla strips fry evenly. They are done when they begin to brown.

Remove the tortillas strips from the heat and place in a bowl. Sprinkle the cheese on top. Place the cooking pot lid over the bowl to retain the heat, and let sit for a couple minutes to let the cheese melt. Serve immediately.

PEANUT BUTTER
PAN COOKIES

Baking cookies while camping is half for the taste and half for the theatrics. "Fresh-baked cookies!" you call out to your friends, and they all come running, ready to stuff their faces. They'll think you've mastered camp cooking, and you'll know just enough to keep them well fooled. With only a few ingredients and even fewer steps, you can make these cookies.

These are based off a pretty simple energy ball recipe, but then fried to bake them, which takes things to a whole new level. Since they require just three fairly basic trip ingredients—oats, peanut butter, and honey—it makes having peanut butter cookies any night of an adventure fairly easy.

The not-so-secret secret ingredient in this recipe is of course the chocolate. Whether it's chocolate chips carefully pulled out of your trail mix, M&M's from your "when things get desperate" stash, or a chocolate bar broken into small pieces, chocolate is really going to make these cookies taste like more than just warm peanut butter.

MAKES 8–10 cookies

INGREDIENTS

½ cup peanut butter, salted (If it's not salted, add a little salt.)

2 tablespoons honey

1 teaspoon cinnamon (optional)

½ cup oats

Handful of some type of chocolaty pieces

PREPARATION

Place the peanut butter, honey, and cinnamon (or any other spices you desire) in a bowl, and use a fork to stir together until well blended. Add the oats and chocolate, and work together until the dough-like mixture holds together.

Break the "dough" into 8 to 10 pieces. Roll each piece into a ball and flatten it.

Place "cookies" in a pan over medium heat and grill for about 1 minute on each side, until they have turned a darker color.

Let cool a bit before serving; you'll burn your mouth if you eat one straight away.

NON-PITA FALAFEL AND PITA
SANDWICHES

Oh, sure, there's pita involved in these sandwiches, but they're not a Pain In The Ass to make. Buy some falafel mix before your trip, fry some up, stuff it in some pita bread, and you've got lunch.

"Who busts out the stove at lunchtime?" you ask. We do. Whoever wrote the No Stoves at Lunch rule didn't know how to live. Plus, as soon as you're done frying up those falafels, put on a pot of water and you'll be ready to brew a post-lunch coffee as soon as you're finished eating.

The only thing about falafel is that it often tastes a little dry. We have the perfect solution for that: Fork-Smashed Hummus (page 46). Fill your pita breads with the two and you'll be set for whatever adventures the afternoon brings.

Since you're not about to do any deep-frying in the backcountry, the easiest way to fry up falafel is to form it into patties as opposed to balls. This makes them easier to flip and ensures that they get fully cooked. Looks don't matter here; you're just going to stuff them in some pita bread. If you're looking to boost the flavor of the falafel (because sometimes the mixes can be bland), consider adding dried red pepper or finely chopped garlic to the mix. Then, once you've got your sandwich in hand, douse the whole thing in as much hot sauce as you can stand.

INGREDIENTS

Falafel mix

Pita bread

Fork-Smashed Hummus

Vegetable oil for frying

Hot sauce

OPTIONAL INGREDIENTS FOR FALAFEL

Dried red pepper

Red pepper flakes

Chopped garlic

PREPARATION

Follow the package instructions to prepare the falafel mix.

(If you are missing the instructions, aim for a ratio that's about 3 parts water to 4 parts falafel mix. Stir the mix, water, and whatever additional ingredients you want to add and let sit for about 15 minutes to absorb the water.)

Form the falafel into balls about the size of walnuts and gently press into patties. Place the patties in a pan coated with oil and fry until crisp, about 3 minutes.

Spoon a little hummus into a pita bread, followed by a falafel patty. (If you have made your patties a little big, break them in half to make them fit.) Douse with hot sauce and enjoy.

APRICOT AND PEANUT
QUINOA

Originally inspired by using up a bag of GORP, this dish is sweet and savory, a taste that comes together well with the addition of a few spices. While it takes a little longer to cook than some of the other grains that are common on backcountry trips, quinoa is nutrient rich. Unlike most plant-based foods, it is also a complete protein.

MAKES 2 servings

RATIO FOR COOKING QUINOA 1 part quinoa to 2 parts water

INGREDIENTS

2 cups water

1 cup quinoa

10 dried apricots, chopped

2 teaspoons cumin powder

2 teaspoons ground cinnamon

½ teaspoon salt

½ cup peanuts

PREPARATION

Place all the ingredients except for the peanuts in a pot. Cover the pot, place on the stove, and bring to a boil. Lower the heat a little and cook for an additional 10 to 15 minutes, until the quinoa has expanded and softened. If you need to add more water while the quinoa is cooking, do so.

Remove from the heat; add in the peanuts and stir together. Cover and let sit for 5 minutes before serving.

THE MORALE BOOST
OF TRAVEL-SIZE HOT SAUCE BOTTLES

ANYONE WHO HAS SPENT SIGNIFICANT TIME IN THE BACKCOUNTRY will tell you it's the small things that make it possible to tolerate all the discomforts: a good pair of lightweight flip-flops or camp shoes on a long backpacking trip after tromping dozens of miles with a heavy pack; a small paperback to read in the tent or after dinner; a few minutes to soak tired feet in an ice-cold mountain creek.

Allow me to present another, perhaps the most important, backcountry morale booster of all: small bottles of hot sauce to spice up all that backcountry food.

That's right: Cholula and Tabasco both make 2-ounce bottles specifically designed for travel. Sriracha has licensed a 1.69-ounce travel bottle that fits on a keychain (or in our case, clips to the outside of a backpack). These little miracles can help you survive even the toughest, longest days in the backcountry, no matter how much your feet hurt, how bad the weather gets, or how whiny your backpacking partner happens to be.

Did the temperature drop while you were cooking dinner and now it's all you can do to finish eating without shivering uncontrollably? No problem. Douse your dinner in hot sauce and feel the warmth spread through your capillaries. Dinner didn't turn out exactly how you wanted it to taste? Pour most of a small bottle of hot sauce on it, and now it tastes like hot sauce. Worried about several long days carrying a heavy pack? Hide your travel hot sauce bottle in your Day Four dinner, forget it, and be pleasantly surprised when you find it.

Got bitten by a rattlesnake? Hot sauce actually won't help with that. You should probably go to a hospital as soon as possible. Slipped and fell and compound fractured your tibia? OK, hot sauce actually does have some limitations. To deal with that compound fracture, you're going to need a different book than this one.

If hot sauce is good enough for Beyoncé's bag, it's good enough for my backpack. And it's good enough for yours. No other 2-ounce item will bring you so much happiness in the backcountry. Choose the appropriate hot sauce for your needs, and if it's a small glass bottle, cover it in a couple layers of duct tape to keep it from shattering (and keep it together if it does shatter), and enjoy your trip. Even the blandest backpacking meals become edible with the addition of a little spice. And it's good for your health—studies have found that capsaicin, the compound that makes peppers hot, can kill cancer cells.

If you're worried about having enough hot sauce, definitely make every hiking partner coming on your trip carry their own bottle. If they refuse, doubting that it will be worth the extra weight, convince them or surreptitiously slide a bottle into their backpack when they're not looking. Otherwise you will find yourself in an awkward situation on Day Two or Three when your hot sauce–less partners detect the obvious joy on your face during dinner and ask, "Could I get a little of your hot sauce?" Because you know they will. And that's bullshit.

Do yourself a favor. Pick up a couple travel bottles of hot sauce today and put them in your backpacking cookset for your next trip. If you don't, you run the risk of wondering how much better the trek could have been if dinner had had just a little more kick to it.

—*Brendan*

COCONUT DATE LOGS
FOR WHEN YOU DON'T HAVE A DATE (OR EVEN IF YOU DO)

Nothing impresses a date like a homemade exotic snack. That same snack will also provide for an excellent solution to I've-hit-a-wall-and-I-have-no-one-to-complain-to if you're adventuring solo and it's late in the day. This recipe will do that and more. This DIY dessert was inspired by some coconut-covered dates we saw in a classic hippy-friendly grocery store. The caveat to this recipe is that you need a food processor; a food processor is going to allow you to blend the ingredients together a lot better, and turn the dates and nuts into a sticky paste. That being said, some finely chopped dates and nuts could probably be molded together with your hands to make for a scrappy version.

Dates have a pretty distinct taste on their own, which is why they are a favorite ingredient of people who like to make energy snacks with limited ingredients. You can add some ground cinnamon or cardamom if you want these to have a little extra flavor. If you're adventuring in very hot weather and have pushed these to the bottom of your bag, don't expect them to hold their shape. But who cares? They're sweet, salty, and delicious.

MAKES About 20 logs

INGREDIENTS

1 cup walnuts

1 cup medjool dates

½ teaspoon sea salt

¼ cup shredded unsweetened coconut

PREPARATION

In a food processor, combine the walnuts, medjool dates, and sea salt until the mixture is finely ground and starts to clump together.

Place the shredded coconut in a bowl.

Form the walnut-date mixture into logs, scooping out a little more than 1 teaspoon for each log. Roll each log in the coconut to cover it.

Store in an airtight container.

TASTES FRESH TO ME
FRUIT CRISP

Fruit crisp in a Dutch oven is one thing, but when you're backpacking, you don't have time for that. This is the simplified version, making use of what you have: dried fruit, oats, and honey. It's low frills, high satisfaction, like every good camp recipe should be.

When you heat honey and oil together with the oats, the oats magically crisp up once they are removed from the stove, and they're easy to sprinkle over a batch of Backpacker's Fruit Compote (page 174). You get that soft, sweet taste of the fruit paired with the crunchy, crispy texture of the oats. It's the easiest classy dessert you could cook up on a trip.

The quantities are "about" because by the time you get to making dessert, you're too tired to care about measuring. Unless you drench the oats in oil, you're probably not going to mess it up. Also, note that spices aren't necessary for this recipe, but they certainly don't hurt. Sprinkle in a little cinnamon and ginger if you have it on hand.

INGREDIENTS

1 batch Backpacker's Fruit Compote

About ½ cup oats

About 1 tablespoon honey

About 1 tablespoon oil

Dash of any spices you have on hand (like cinnamon, ginger, or cardamom)

PREPARATION

Prepare a batch of Backpacker's Fruit Compote and set it aside.

In a frying pan over medium heat, combine the oats, honey, oil, and any spices you want. Stir together so that the honey and oil evenly coat the oats. Continue stirring regularly until the oats have turned a dark golden brown.

Remove the mixture from the stove and let sit for a few minutes to cool. The oats will crisp up as they cool.

Sprinkle the oats over the compote and serve.

ACKNOWLEDGMENTS

BRENDAN'S ACKNOWLEDGMENTS

Thanks to my friends Teresa Bruffey, Jayson Sime, and Erik Wardell for contributing recipes to this book.

Thanks to Mitsu Iwasaki for teaching me that you don't have to eat crappy-tasting food just because you're miles from civilization, and that a little effort goes a long way out there.

Thanks to all my friends who put up with my less-than-fantastic backcountry food experiments in the years prior to writing this book.

And thanks to Anna Brones for saying yes to this idea when I asked her. I think we both know that this book would have been terrible without her (or would have not existed at all).

ANNA'S ACKNOWLEDGMENTS

Thanks to Luc Revel for playing extra photographer and hand model, even after a French press fiasco.

Thanks to my father, Norman Brones, for teaching me at a very early age that getting outside was important, and later in life, serving as a test bunny for plenty of outdoor meals.

And thanks to Brendan Leonard for thinking that I was worthy enough to take on a project with him. I'm happy that he believes in coffee breaks as much as I do.

APPENDIX

APPROXIMATE U.S. METRIC EQUIVALENTS

LIQUID INGREDIENTS

U.S. MEASURES	METRIC	U.S. MEASURES	METRIC
¼ tsp.	1.23 ml	2 Tbsp.	29.57 ml
½ tsp.	2.36 ml	3 Tbsp.	44.36 ml
¾ tsp.	3.70 ml	¼ cup	59.15 ml
1 tsp.	4.93 ml	½ cup	118.30 ml
1¼ tsp.	6.16 ml	1 cup	236.59 ml
1½ tsp.	7.39 ml	2 cups or 1 pt.	473.18 ml
1¾ tsp.	8.63 ml	3 cups	709.77 ml
2 tsp.	9.86 ml	4 cups or 1 qt.	946.36 ml
1 Tbsp.	14.79 ml	4 qts. or 1 gal.	3.79 l

DRY INGREDIENTS

U.S. MEASURES	METRIC	U.S. MEASURES		METRIC
¹⁄₁₆ oz.	2 (1.8) g	2⅘ oz.		80 g
⅛ oz.	3½ (3.5) g	3 oz.		85 (84.9) g
¼ oz.	7 (7.1) g	3½ oz.		100 g
½ oz.	15 (14.2) g	4 oz.		115 (113.2) g
¾ oz.	21 (21.3) g	4½ oz.		125 G
⅞ oz.	25 g	5¼ oz.		150 g
1 oz.	30 (28.3) g	8⅞ oz.		250 g
1¾ oz.	50 g	16 oz.	1 lb.	454 g
2 oz.	60 (56.6) g	17⅗ oz.	1 livre	500 g

RESOURCES

Shopping for adventure-friendly foods isn't always easy if your local grocery store isn't fully stocked. Here is a list of resources for dehydrated foods and ingredients. We believe in whole ingredients and real food, and these companies do too.

Alpine Aire: https://www.alpineaire.com

Good to Go: https://goodto-go.com/

Harmony House: http://www.harmonyhousefoods.com/

Heather's Choice: https://www.heatherschoice.com

Karen's Naturals Just Veggies: https://www.shopkarensnaturals.com

Outdoor Herbivore: https://outdoorherbivore.com

Packit Gourmet: http://www.packitgourmet.com/

Patagonia Provisions: https://www.patagoniaprovisions.com/

INDEX

ABOUT THE AUTHORS

Denver-based **BRENDAN LEONARD** is the creator of Semi-Rad.com, and his writing has appeared in *Climbing, Alpinist, Backpacker, Outside, Adventure Cyclist, Sierra, National Geographic Adventure,* and dozens of other publications. He is the author of several books, including *Sixty Meters to Anywhere, The Great Outdoors: A User's Guide, Classic Front Range Trad Climbs,* and *Make It Till You Make It.*

ANNA BRONES is the founder of FoodieUnderground.com and Comestible, and her work has been featured in the *New York Times, Adventure Cyclist, Adventure Journal, The Guardian, The Kitchn,* and many other publications. Pacific Northwest-based, she is the author of several books, including *The Culinary Cyclist, Fika: The Art of the Swedish Coffee Break, Paris Coffee Revolution,* and *Hello, Bicycle: An Inspired Guide to the Two-Wheeled Life.*